On that day in 2012, I had my new professional goal: help people who were in search of the knowledge that I had been seeking out for the first ten years of my career. So, what was my sales/professional philosophy? I came back to the two things I was good at, or at least I thought I was good at. Playing golf and hanging out in establishments that served adult beverages. Honestly, I love golf, but there have been so many comparisons between business and golf even I was sick of them. I thought about comparisons between bar life and the business world, and it clicked. I literally have been hanging out in bars since I was nine years old, not drinking, but watching games, playing hoop shot, and hanging out with my uncles and cousins after their softball and football games. After playing on the PGA Tour, opening life. The bar remains one of my favorite made me miss that environment, and I returning to some sort of normalcy. Th packed bars. I have always preferred div  that allow for some level of conversation. Places without VIPs and bottle service. Give me bad lighting, cheesy décor, and good people; this is my "happy place."

I openly admit I don't know it all; this is just my take on how to be successful in a "dog eats dog" world. Since the first draft of this book, I have gone on to run the global commercial team at a diagnostic company that conducts business in 27 countries, I have started and managed my own consulting firm, and I have been the Chief Commercial Officer to a well-funded medical startup. I have sold and won in highly technical, highly competitive markets. I have been turned down for jobs that should have been mine and been given jobs that I wasn't ready for. Although this doesn't make me a master of the universe, I do think I can help some of you. This is not a drinking book; you do not need to be friends with Jack, José, or Johnny to get something out of it. However, you do have to know what the inside of a bar looks like.

The bar remains a place where people from different cultures, socioeconomic statuses, and ages can enjoy each other's company with few preconditions. In my travels, I have been to bars in Asia, Europe, and North America. They all have the same basic ground rules and if you understand them, you can have a carefree good time and come away with some tremendous stories. There is a unique comradery in pubs that I truly enjoy, and when the pandemic took that away, I think society suffered. The bar is obviously not nirvana; there are some negatives that often cannot be avoided, but nothing in this world is perfect.

Again, please have some fun with this. My favorite days at work are the days that I come home and tell my wife, "Damn that was fun!" I say the same thing after a good night at the bar with my favorite people.

# About the Author

**Doug Gentilcore** started his career about as far from the boardroom as you can imagine. As a golf professional in Scarsdale, NY, he had aspirations of battling Tiger Woods on the PGA Tour. That dream was short-lived and soon he began his sales career with a business-to-business role in Annapolis, MD. Even though Doug's professional golf career is long over, competition on the course, on the field, and in the business arena continues to be a defining part of his life.

As Doug's career advanced, he had stops at Pfizer and GE, which helped build a foundation for his success in sales, and where he began to develop his theories on sales and marketing. As Doug rose through the management ranks, he gained a deeper understanding of why his customers were motivated to buy from him. Doug's growth and performance eventually led to him leading commercial teams on a global level.

Doug has since founded Implerem, LLC and has worked with and for several organizations, helping them with strategy and commercialization. Whether it was large companies like Novartis, private equity firms like Bain Capital, or small organizations like ARTMS Products Inc., Doug found that having strong principles, strategy and finding people who can execute at a high level were all critically important success factors. Recently, Doug became the Chief Commercial Officer at ARTMS Products Inc., an exciting new medical technology still in its funding phase. Implerem continues to serve customers with the principles established by Doug. Doug continues his consulting in a limited role while working with clients in unrelated industries.

Doug's true passion is helping people grow and maximize their potential. He was fortunate to have an exceptional group of mentors and advocates during his career, and he will continue to use his platform to help as many business professionals as possible. Whether it comes from his writing, speaking, or customer relationships, Doug's first priority is to make those around him the best version of themselves.

Doug is backed by an incredibly supportive wife, children, and extended family that have all had an immense impact on his life.

# Introduction

It's mid-morning of a random August 2003 day in Orlando, FL. The first thing I feel is my head pounding from whatever damage I had done to my body the previous evening. Then, as I slowly open my groggy eyes and look around an apartment that is not mine, I say to myself, "I'm done with this madness, it's time to act like a grown-up." The "madness" I spoke of was pursuing a professional golf career. There was a sense of relief when I decided to abandon my dream of playing on the PGA Tour because, well, I was nowhere close to good enough at golf. The feeling that came to me next is something I will never forget. What in the hell am I going to do now?!?!?

I had a degree, a supportive family, and little else. The credit card that I had used to fund my pursuits was maxed out and I had roughly $37 in my bank account. Needless to say, I didn't have the money to start my own business and even if I did, I didn't have any good ideas! I had some job prospects back home and a few college friends who had worked themselves into good jobs with big companies. There certainly wasn't a job waiting for me at home, and I didn't really even know where to get started. I did know that my life was about to drastically change, and I was convinced the decision to stop pursuing my dream of playing golf professionally meant that all of the fun as I knew it was over.

When I arrived back home in Maryland, I was defeated and embarrassed. I thought everyone would see me as a failure, and who wants to give a loser a job? After some empty meetings and phone calls, I was given a lifeline by one of my Uncle Chris's clients, Larry Reagan. Larry said, "You should come sell for me!" And the rest, as they say, is history.

Many of you have found yourselves in relatable circumstances. You know that something needs to change, but the question is, what? Over the next 25 chapters of this book, you will hear stories about my experiences, advice on your career, and how they can help you be or become a better business person, sales professional, and maybe even friend or significant other. Your experiences will certainly be different than mine; for the younger readers it will be apparent that when I was a younger man, I did not have to manage through a global pandemic, social media, and a 24-hour news cycle. However, unlike a number of training and management programs I have been through, you will walk away with real-life parallels that will help you handle the unique situations you will face on a daily basis.

Nearly everyone has come to a point in their life and career where we just didn't know what to do in a given situation. It is at these times that your founding principles are critically important to act as your guide. Without a clear understanding of what you believe and why, your chances of accomplishing your goal significantly decrease.

Many of the valuable lessons I have learned took place in social settings, specifically in establishments whose main business was serving adult beverages, or in much simpler terms, in bars. Growing up in the Baltimore-Washington area allowed me to experience a number of events in a variety of settings, many of which will be discussed in the following pages. Again, they are my anecdotes and they have provided the foundation that has played a major role in my successes. They have also helped me deal with challenges and even more importantly with my failures, of which there are many. Whether I won or lost a deal, the principles that I developed from social settings continue to provide clarity and focus when it is most needed. The purpose and hope of this book is to help you find commonalities and then establish your core values in business and in life moving forward.

Please understand that I have been in your position, and I would be skeptical as well. Most of the business, sales, and self-improvement books that I have read early in my career were thrust upon me by a boss or a mentor. Frankly, I had no interest in reading any of them, but today I can say with certainty that I am glad these people forced me to read these authors' words. So feel free to start this manuscript with a dismissive tone, I am confident I will win you over. It may not be immediately, but in the near future, you will find yourself in a spot where something in this book will help you maneuver and even thrive when you thought neither was possible.

While I do not like asking or doing favors for people I do not know, I am going to ask you to do three things before you start on the journey of the chapters to follow:

First, you have to put in some work to get the most out of this book. Please understand that this is not a manual to success; this is the start of your journey to establish your philosophy on business and perhaps even your personal life. You will find stories that you can relate to, others will leave you wondering why, and some may even cause you to cringe. There are things in my past that bring me a massive sense of pride and others that make me want to crawl under a rock. They are all important! So, put in the work and be honest with your self-evaluations along the way.

Second, keep an open mind. I have read and been through trainings that I knew weren't going to be successful: The trainer was ill-equipped, or their philosophy was flawed. The speaker or author had no chance of teaching me anything, because I never gave them the chance. I request that you don't repeat my mistake. That being said, even when I took my most closed-minded stance, I still managed to take away useful items from the book or training that I gave virtually no chance to positively impact me. So, feel free to write and tell me that you "got nothing out of this," with one caveat. When I write you back six months later, you concede that you did use one of these lessons and it did indeed help you manage through a time that lacked clarity. Deal?

My final request is to have some fun with this publication. I certainly enjoyed writing it and living these stories provided more than a little amusement. You don't need me to tell you this, but life is not always a pleasure, and you have to embrace the good moments. I don't take myself too seriously, even though there are a number of people that depend on me delivering results, family included. I will tell you that none of the hard work and sacrifice is worth it, if you don't enjoy yourself along the way.

Let's get this ball rolling. I'm ready if you are.

# 1

## *Have Your Credentials at the Door*

Everyone knows that you need ID to legally be in a bar. When you think about it, it took you 21 years to get into that bar! It won't take you 21 years to make a sale; if it does, you will never see that sale through to the end. I know what you are thinking: "I got into a bar way before my 21st birthday." Well, so did I. We all found some form of entry. We either knew someone at the door or had (ahem) alternative identification. Either way you look at it, you had to have some type of credential to get in the door; some of us were just better at it than others. If any of you have been fortunate enough to be a VIP or be "on the list," you know that this brings you a different level of access and that it can lead to some amazing things. In my experience, you become a VIP in two ways: you can pay for it, or you bring something to that bar or club that no one else does. Being that I was never a rich kid, I couldn't afford to pay my way in, so I had to bring something unique to the table. That something varied from situation to situation, and it forced me to be creative to achieve my very basic goal of getting into the bar.

There is a direct correlation to your sales life—make sure you have ID with you. Knowledge is the most powerful credential you can bring in the business world. As much as I poke fun at my training in the opening, all of that training and product knowledge is essential. You need to collect the data, know everything your competition is going to emphasize to your customer, and know why that is actually an advantage for your service or product. Do not limit yourself to what your company gives you for training; make sure you speak to your customers. I mean all of your customers, from the entry-level staffer to the senior administrator. If the person is anywhere near your market, talk to them about your products and company. If you don't have a baseline understanding of your products,

DOI: 10.4324/9781003218258-1

you are no good to anyone, especially yourself. That being said, you don't need to know everything about your products and market to sell your product. I have seen it done and done it; once you have a baseline, you can sell anything. Remember, there is nothing wrong with telling your customer, "Hey, I'm brand new and I don't have all the answers yet, but our service has demonstrated that it brings them x, y, and z; based on what you have told me and what I have read about you and your team, it may do the same for you." You can have a limited base of knowledge and bring a high level of value to your customer. One thing is critically important to remember: do not make it up as you go! Credibility is hard to gain and easy to lose, just like trust. Once the customer believes you are full of it and present little to no value, they will most likely take a long time, if ever to work with you. There is nothing wrong with saying, "I am not sure, but I will follow up with you via email or next time I am in the area."

I have been around some people with truly amazing product knowledge. I mean a level of knowledge I wouldn't reach in three lifetimes and not have any clue on how to use all of that knowledge to influence their customers. A big part of the credentialing process is researching who you are dealing with and what makes them tick. The Internet is an invaluable resource. You have a one-stop shop to find mission statements, C-suite personnel, and organizational history. It is almost disturbing how much you can find out about your customer via the web. This can lead to a potential issue; I have gone into meetings thinking I knew so much about a customer that I forgot to ask them. This is a big problem. It is fine to interject with, "I think I read that about your company," but no one wants to be undressed by the Internet. Ask open-ended questions that align with your customer's values, mission statement, or stated goals. Never assume you know your customer, let them educate you.

Make sure you roll up your sleeves, get into an organization, and speak to the entire cast of characters. Ask to come in and observe their organization, not only will it give you a chance to build a relationship with the customer, but you will learn more about the future of the organization than you will ever see online. Would an organization put a five-year capital replacement plan online? Perhaps, but you may get the uncensored version if you have a relationship with your customer. As you establish your credibility with the client, they are more likely to give you their list of priorities and allow you to move your product up the list. You can only get this type of access if you show proper "ID" with the customer, they may even make you a

VIP! The part that is overlooked by so many sales professionals is to really understand where the market is going and how it relates to your customer and your products. Unless you have a good sense of the challenges and opportunities that your client will encounter, it is near impossible to properly position your portfolio. This has been given so many names: "seeing the field," "looking around the corner," and, my personal favorite, "being strategic." These are things I have spoken about during every single interview I have ever been on. Mainly because I have always been asked, "Are you a strategic thinker? Can you give me an example? Of course, I can, uh, uh, uh, I once had a customer who needed to buy paper from me, but I also noticed that he needed paperclips. So, I brought in my paperclip guy, and we put a strategic contract agreement together to buy both items from us for one year." Wow, I really blew them away on that one, aren't you impressed? The most strategic thinkers I have seen focus very little on product and very heavily on the market and trends.

I think being strategic is the hardest part of the credentialing process. I still strive to be market-focused or strategic every day. It is very easy to focus on your deal and pull the old "let me get this one done, and I will get strategic on the next one" approach to selling. And honestly, sometimes large-scale strategic planning just isn't reasonable, but it should always be the goal. Strategic thinking is an art, and I have only seen a few people get it right. All of the most successful people I have worked with and for demonstrate an ability to see around the corner on every deal. Almost anyone can hit it out of the park from time to time. The truly dynamic businesspeople live with a strategic mindset. They ask questions like, "What does this deal mean to my customer's brand and market? What is the next opportunity that will present after I win this deal and how can I utilize this win for others?"

This is not about age; this is about a mindset. Just because someone is 60+ and has been around for 25 years doesn't automatically make him a master of the market. In my experience, most people that have stayed in the same company for 25 years tend to be more task-oriented. You can make a very good living by being a taskmaster, and there is absolutely nothing wrong with it. Again, it is important not to make any assumptions. You will also find that certain people stay in one place because they believe and love what they do every day. Our goal here is to avoid being task-oriented and to understand that no deal or customer exists in a silo; there is always a secondary or new deal that will come from your wins, and losses.

I used to think that being strategic meant getting customers to sign long-term agreements over multiple market segments with my company. This was a good start, but when things really started happening was when I tied market knowledge with macroeconomic understanding and political happenings. I needed to understand how each of these played off one another to truly see this field that many people have been telling me about. I was never really into politics, but I did major in economics and had bought into the market side of business. So, I begrudgingly watched all of the channels my dad watched in his living room, which I had deemed the "oval office." I dug in: CNN, Fox News, and MSNBC were now in the mix. I wanted to get all sides of the equation, so I sought out new information every chance I got. Whether it was right-wing or left-wing, I listened, I judged, I absorbed. It was boring and I still found myself switching to ESPN every chance I got. I still do this to give me perspective, but how does this help strategic thinking?

The things that were happening adjacent to me had a direct impact on my business and were important. Whether they knew it or not, every single one of these actions had an impact on my customers, which was more important. I can be a liberal or a conservative at the drop of a hat, this is the skill you should have as well. I do everything in my power to avoid political opinions in my business interactions, but I do frequently discuss what the government is doing and how it may affect the market I am working in. I really don't care what your political views are, but you should realize the government will either be your number one customer or the number one influence on your customer. You need to know what is going on politically and the potential impact of those actions. I will warn you: even though politics are important, you are walking a very fine line when you bring the government into a business discussion. Proceed with caution and if you can avoid it, please do so.

If you can bring your market, macroeconomics, and the government into your selling you are truly being strategic. Let me expand on that. The highest members of the corporate food chain reside in the C-suite. Now they may have to approve some of your deals, but they really aren't concerned about your specific product, even if they are spending five million dollars with you. They are buying from you to satisfy a market need, remain competitive, or differentiate within the market. They have surveyed the rules of the game laid out by the government and make their moves based on the economic impact anticipated from these rules.

I honestly thought that a CEO cared about my product, but they didn't. They cared what my product would do to help them position themselves in the market. The great part about strategic thinking is that it is scalable, and the principles can be used from the bottom up. Every decision-maker along the way will be influenced by your strategic messaging.

I mentioned earlier that you had two ways to become a VIP: either pay for it or bring something to the table that is truly special. I never have and never will pay for it, and neither should you. Paying for it is for lazy people and at some point, the money will run out, leaving you with an empty wallet and out on your ass with another "pay for play" clown in your place. Demonstrate some value and be strategic if you want to be "on the list." Let me be clear; sometimes you will have to move your price to win the deal, and this is ok. That being said, it should be the very last thing you do, and it should never be significant enough to devalue your product or market. Also, when you give up some price, make sure you get something of value in return. Wins come and go; value creation is long-lasting and sustainable.

It is a simple rule, but if you don't have the proper credentials, you aren't going anywhere in this world. It was up to you to figure out the best way to get into the bar. It is now up to you to earn enough credibility to get that job when you have little experience, or close that highly competitive deal. Chances are if you can get in the door, you have what it takes to be a VIP. The question is will you put in the work?

# 2

## Have an In

In every major metropolitan area, there are always clubs that are THE spot to be and near impossible to gain entry. You can tell which one by the ridiculously long lines and notoriously difficult doormen. Inevitably, while you are waiting in line, there is a group of people who walk right to the front with a hug or handshake with the doorman and stroll right into the bar, while the rest of the people wait for their turn, which often never comes. I have been on both sides of this equation, and I have to admit that I prefer not waiting in line. In your professional life, you will often feel like you are in the back of the line behind your competition, wishing you had a way to move up in the pecking order. I rarely use the word always, but in this case, it is always better to know who guards the door to your deal, and if they are your "in," your chances of winning skyrocket. So, the question is, how? How do you make a connection that gives you an unfair advantage over your competition? How do you differentiate yourself from the crowd? How do you create your "in" with the customer everyone is fighting over? There is no hard and fast rule, and you have to work hard to earn it.

Often a customer will ask for an RFP or Request for Proposal from multiple vendors for a given product or service. In my experience, this can go one of two ways and one is certainly highly preferred to the other. In the first scenario, you get a call or email informing you that this process has begun, and you have to submit your proposal in a specific format at a specific time, and the client will not engage in any unstructured discussion. In the second scenario, you get a call from your customer telling you when the RFP will go out, what they are looking for, and what you can do to differentiate yourself from the competitors. Needless to say, I prefer the latter option. So how do you get there? The answer is painfully simple and difficult to attain at the same time.

DOI: 10.4324/9781003218258-2

I have been told my entire life that relationships are the key to opening doors for yourself or that it's all "who you know." While I partially agree with this logic, I have found that productive relationships are what truly open doors and are less about who you know and more about what you bring to the table. In other words, the difference lies in what level of value you create. That doorman isn't playing favorites at random; he either knows the people who are cutting the line, or they are bringing something to the table you aren't. Your customer will treat you the same way as that doorman if you don't show value; you will be in line with the other cast of characters waiting for your turn, which may never come. Building a relationship is more than being able to engage in small talk with your customer, more than remembering their kids' names. That is part of it for some of your customers; others could not care less about that kind of interaction. Bringing value is the universal way to gain preferred access to your customer and potential deals. There is no magic formula for creating value; however, there are some hard and fast rules that I have found to create value for your customer. First, know who the customer "doorman" is for your deal. While I believe in forging professional bonds with as many people as possible who are involved in the deal, you need to know who owns your access. The only way to do this is to ask questions about the process to understand who makes what decision and when. We all have at least one boss, know who holds the keys to the deal, and start building.

Second, be a follow-up champion. If the customer asks you for something, follow up with exactly what they want in a timely manner. Their request has to become your number one priority; if you can't fulfill that request in the timeline that the customer has given to you, tell him that. Think about it: if you are interested in hiring a contractor for your house and the quality of their work and price are similar, are you more likely to work with the contractor that always responds to emails, texts, and calls, or the one that takes nine days to return a text? It's an easy decision for you, and if you don't follow up emphatically, it will be an easy decision for your potential customer.

Finally, be an educator. If you are seen as a knowledgeable person and you can share that knowledge effectively, you will be seen as a resource by your prospective client. Make sure you speak to their goals, not yours. If you don't know what their mission is, ask them. You will be surprised how much information your customer will share if you ask, "What goals have you laid out for your organization this quarter/year?" Once you understand what they are trying to accomplish, you can tailor your message to help them reach those stated goals. If the customer's goals don't directly align with yours, make adjustments and be patient with your messaging. No salesperson has rushed to squeeze in their messaging and seen high levels of success. There is no magic potion, the secret is in the work. Put in the work and you will gain the respect of your customer.

If you have a relationship with the people at the "door," you will get that preferred access that we all desire. Once you are in the bar, you have a whole new world in front of you. There is a group who has access to what you really want—they are the bartenders. When you are in the bar, you are at their mercy. You can sit there all night and not get a drink, you can sit and wait in line just like you did at the door, or you can be the person the bartender seeks out and says, "Good to see you again. What can I get for you?"

The doormen in the business world tend to be mid-level managers or key lower-level workers. The bartenders are the final decision-makers, the C-suite personnel, the purchasing directors, and the board members. That is not to say you now ignore the doorman, but the bartenders hold the keys to what you really want. Your interaction with the bartenders/final decision-makers is different than the doormen. This interaction is more transactional: you have a product, they have money, and at some point, these two items meet and then change hands.

Your selling approach will change with these players. More likely than not cost will play a large part in the discussion. It is important to either have the mid-level managers (doorman) in your meetings or give the final decision-makers their input on why your product or service is best for the organization. You can have a great message, but it is much more impactful to have someone from inside deliver that message for you. If you have sold your customer on your product before the pricing discussion takes place, you are exactly where you want to be in the deal process. The bartender group will try to squeeze you and try to dazzle you with fancy acronyms like TCO (total cost of ownership) and make thinly veiled threats about your competition's offer. At the end of the day, bartenders really don't care if their organization buys your product or your competition's product. They do, however, want to keep their people (doormen) happy and stay competitive in their market.

When dealing with the bartenders or C-suite, it is important to ask what their goals are to see if they align with the "doorman" goals. Chances are they will be related but not exactly the same. The "bartender" goals will be broader in nature and focused on long-term growth or strategic imperatives. It is important to remain composed in your meetings with these types of customers. Have you ever lost your cool with a bartender in a pub? If so, how did that turn out for you? I know you didn't get a drink, and most likely your evening ended early.

Building a relationship with final decision-makers is much different than your mid-level personnel; it is more difficult to get close to them. Just like the bartender, there is always a barrier between you and them. The thing to remember is if you can form a productive relationship with the final decision-maker (bartender), the rewards are numerous and large in scale. It is a beautiful thing to have an "open tab" from a bartender; imagine having an "open tab" with the CEO of a multi-million-dollar organization. Those types of relationships put your kids through private school and help you retire when you're young enough to enjoy it.

The only way to "have an in" with the final decision-makers is to exceed their expectations. I'm not talking smoke and mirrors or showering them with gifts. I am talking about respect and credibility; you must at least meet their requirements, and you and your product need to over-deliver. You have to speak their language and assist them in reaching their organizational goals. These relationships are the most valuable you can make in your career. It is important to not over-promise with this group. If you set unrealistic expectations here, you will be held to them, and they will be an anchor around your neck for as long as you have this customer under contract.

Now, there are times when you will not have your "in," and you should still win. If you find yourself in line with your competitors, you need to differentiate every chance you get. Do not bash your competition. You have no idea who your competitors have relationships with within that organization. You could find yourself in a really tough spot by doing this; focus on what you and your service/product do well. Be a master to the process that is in front of you, meaning you need to know how, when, and who will buy. Over-prepare—if you are not fully prepared, you will give the customer an excuse to dismiss you, your message, and your product. If you come up short on handouts or have computer issues, you have put an unnecessary burden on yourself, and the deal will be in jeopardy. In a highly competitive bid process, there is one thing that will pull the customer in your direction. The customer will give you keys on what that one thing is; keep your eyes and ears open and you will see it. Once you find that key deciding factor, you have to make sure to always come back to it. Even if you are talking about something unrelated, like a product warranty, find a way to bring up that one thing during the discussion; it should be burned into your customer's brain. Don't forget it's the small things that make the difference and being prepared helps you accomplish cover the small details that lead to big wins.

It is always best to have an "in," both at the door and at the bar. Your life will be much easier if you have the groundwork laid out to cut in front of your competition in line. If you aren't connected yet with your customer, don't freak out; you just have to outwork and outsmart your competition. You can do it!

# 3

## *Set the Agenda for the Evening*

Whether it is just you and a friend or a large gathering, it is always better to have a reason to be out at the bar versus just going out to go out. If you are in the bar for no apparent reason at all, you really need to take a deep look inside and figure out what you are doing with your life. When it comes to setting the agenda for the evening, you can certainly be the one organizing the events for the evening, but it is better if it is mutually agreed upon by the group. When the entire party is out for the same reason, it usually leads to a fun night.

It can be to celebrate a birthday, an anniversary, or just to get together with old friends, but there has to be some reason for leaving your couch and television. This is just as important when you are going to meet with your customer. They are busy people; if they aren't busy then they most likely aren't ready or can't buy anything. When a salesperson makes a call, they are asking the customer to stop their day and give you a few moments of their precious time. Now, you can either make it very clear upfront or get to why you are there in the course of the meeting; either way, a goal must be set.

There is no such thing as just stopping by. Be there for a reason or don't show up. You should always have a goal, but you also can't be a slave to it. You have to be flexible enough to let your customer reach their agenda as well. You wouldn't stop two members of your party from having a good time if they weren't having fun the way you wanted them to, would you? Set the agenda, but make sure you leave some room to please the crowd. Remember, it is possible and highly preferred that both you and your customer achieve the goals that are most important to each party.

When I say set an agenda, I really mean determine the goal for each time you see your customer. Know where you want to take them. Are you

DOI: 10.4324/9781003218258-3

looking to close the deal or are you just trying to open the door to another meeting? Be aware that you must make sure that your agenda is realistic. If you are going out with a group of friends to watch the Super Bowl, you can't expect to be given tickets to the game by the bartender. If you are meeting with a customer for an introduction and product review, your goal can't be to close a million-dollar deal on the first call. This works the other way as well. A goal that is easy to reach is underachieving and worse than asking for too much. If your customer is ready to buy and all you want to do is have a check-the-box status update meeting, you are missing the boat. Set aggressive meeting goals, but make sure you have a chance of meeting those goals.

The difficult part is determining what a reasonable goal is without selling yourself short. The key to this concept is having an understanding of your customer's agenda and speaking in those terms. If your customer is looking to buy apples and you are selling oranges, you are going to get nowhere fast. You need to know what your customer's agenda is for that day, year, or even decade. You can't overpower your customer by asking them to ignore their goals because yours are more important. It would be like going out with friends and dictating what they are drinking for the night, no one wins in that type of scenario.

So, how do we find out what our customer's goals are? Not to be painfully obvious, but you can ask them. Questions are the most powerful tool at your disposal, I always sit back in amazement of businesspeople who know how and what questions to ask. I have noticed that the questions are never yes/no, they are always open-ended. Good salespeople never interrupt an answer to insert a message either, let the customer talk themselves into the proverbial corner and then you can start to respond while layering in your messaging. Think about it, the question to your friends isn't "Do you want to go out?" It is "Where should we go tonight?" In the business world, it shouldn't be "Does this product/service interest you?" It should be "How could this product/service play a role in your day-to-day business?" Also, don't forget the internet. As previously stated, it is an unending source of information. You may have to dig and spend some of your precious "off time" (it's in quotes, because there is no such thing), but if you put in the work, you can find plenty of helpful information to assist you in closing the deal.

As we come back to setting the agenda, you must strike a balance between keeping your customer on the agenda while respecting but pushing their priorities further down the road. There are two approaches here; the first is to convince the customer that even though their agenda is important, yours needs to take precedent. This is definitely the more difficult road, and you better have something the customer absolutely cannot live without, or you will be dismissed quickly. Your product or service needs to be unique, innovative, and without any major flaw or you will alienate that person who ignored their personal agenda and gave their time to your agenda. Even if your product is life-changing, you still must respect your client's priorities. Think about the products you use in your life daily, like your iPhone. I vividly remember colleagues telling me that they were never getting rid of their Blackberry, and they would have no use for a touch screen and "whatever an app is." Those people had no clue what a revelation (and curse at times) a smartphone would be, and they most likely live on their smartphone now. In this instance, new technology was not a priority for my colleagues; until they saw others utilize innovations to improve their work and life, they had no interest. If you try to shove your agenda down your client's throat, it will come back your way in a very negative sense.

In order to set the agenda, your sell will have to be passionate and aggressive; think about a time when you really wanted to go to a certain bar or club and your friend wanted to go another way. How did you convince him or her to go to your bar? My guess is you really stepped up your game and gave an impassioned pitch. Your argument was based on more than "I want to go to Bar X because it is awesome!" You gave your pitch about the high quality of the drinks, the ratio of members of the opposite sex, and the fantastic music. You believed in your heart this was the best place to go and made sure you set the agenda. In order to completely replace your customer's priorities for yours, the same passion and enthusiasm will need to be deployed. You will have to be willing to stand on that island and live with the repercussions if you want to completely upset the apple cart.

The second approach is a little more refined, more consultative, and will probably lead to more success. In this approach, you need to speak to your customer about why your particular good or service helps the customer reach their agenda. The customer either doesn't recognize or doesn't believe your product is part of the solution; if they did, you would be the agenda. You need to speak to your customer as if your product or service can play an integral role in helping them reach their goal. You are creating need in this approach by opening the customer's eyes to a new market or strategy. In an ideal world, you would want your customer to tell you how your product helps them reach their goals. Make sure you don't stop your customer if they find a new use for your product. If you've done your job, the customer will take you down this path, don't get in the way. It is important to remember here that the customer's priority becomes your priority, and your product helps your client reach their goals, not the other way around. Do not lose sight of your customer's priorities, regardless of your approach to setting the agenda.

I am sure you have had a friend who wanted to meet his next special someone or find a place to hear great music that particular evening. You have a place in mind for both and it happens to be the place you want to go that night. When you bring this up to your friend, you talk about how conducive the bar was to striking up conversations with new people or the fact they have a house DJ that is amazing. You have framed the evening's agenda around your friend's goal; now everybody wins. The important thing is that you understood your friend's agenda before you began proposing solutions. Again, ask the questions and never assume the answers.

So always make sure that there is an agenda and goals for your customer interactions. The agenda must be aggressive, but also reasonable and attainable.

# 4

## Make Sure Everyone Has a Drink

After the agenda has been set, you need to make sure everyone has what they need to accomplish the stated goals. Isn't the first thing you do when you walk into a bar is look at your friends and ask, "What do you want?" Chances are you get a variety of answers, the low-maintenance beer, the mid-level vodka/soda, and the high-maintenance cocktail that comes out in some sort of novelty bowl and looks like something my grandmother would have in her garden.

You should essentially ask your customer the same question: "What do you need to accomplish your goals?" or "What would help you solve your organization's issues?" They will give you information if you ask. You will get a variety of answers here as well; some of them may be a test or a smokescreen, but the questions still must be asked. If you don't ask, it would be like ordering a drink for a complete stranger. You might get lucky and guess right, but most likely they will just placate you and then move on as soon as possible.

As the one who sets the agenda, you now become the de facto host for the evening, and now that everyone is drinking, you have to do your best within reason to fulfill their needs. Now every once in a while, you will come across the guy who wants the Crystal or the Dom. It is very important you make it clear to the person who expects too much that there is no way you will be able to live up to that, and then you begin to compromise.

When you are dealing with someone who expects so much because they are important and feel they deserve everything, you need to figure out how to neutralize the situation. Once you have the "person who wants it all and then some" neutralized, they will allow the deal to go through even if they didn't get everything they wanted. For instance, you are dealing with a customer's office manager who loves to beat up on salespeople. They

DOI: 10.4324/9781003218258-4

ask for everything free and expect the best pricing you have ever given to anyone else, plus a 10% additional discount, because they are special. This type of person is obviously enjoying their power trip and wants to see how far he can push the salesperson who they automatically assume is completely full of it. One of my favorite lines for this type of character is, "You and I both know I can never give you everything you want and ask for, but what I can do is deliver what I say I will deliver." This gives you the power to say no, but also lets the customer know you are someone who can be trusted, and if you don't deliver, they have the right to stick it to you. When dealing with a client with unreasonable expectations, it is important to have them prioritize their list of demands and then you can set expectations on what you can deliver and when.

Conversely, there is always someone you would love to wine and dine with who orders an iced tea when you actually want him to break the bank. It is my experience that this person is either being cautious and doesn't quite trust you yet or he is overly timid and will never accept the invite to blow up your bar bill. You can learn a lot from this type of customer; if he is being cautious, you have not done enough to gain his trust. Maybe you have not been genuine, or you have taken him for granted and now he feels you are trying to "buy" his affection. If you are at this stage, you need to retrace your steps and make sure your pitch is matching the customer's agenda. Have you been pushing them in a direction they didn't want to go? Do you have your "in" yet or are you still "waiting in line?" Either way, you still have a lot of work to do, and you have to take a step back before you try to move forward.

If your customer is timid, this will tell you a lot about how you need to sell to them. This type of customer will not respond to your high-energy sales presentation and over-the-top antics. You need to pump the brakes a bit around this customer. This type of customer is the least likely to commit to one vendor; they always like to spread it around and give everyone a taste. They do not respond well to negative comments about your competition, so don't bash. Again, don't ever bash your competition. Tell them what your company can do, tell them that your competition can't do the same thing, but don't ever insult their character or products. The timid or appeasing customer will force you to develop a long, tenuous relationship if you want the bulk of their business. And even if you do get the majority of their business, they will always entertain your competitor's advances. It is enough to make you beat your head against the wall, but it is part of the game with this type of customer. The upside here is, for the most part, these are the type of customers that have the most buying power within an organization. Their cautious nature reflects well on them, and their bosses are likely to trust this person's opinion on products and vendors.

The most difficult thing to do while you are getting everyone their "drinks" is to keep your goal in mind and make sure you are still working toward it. When you are addressing your customer's needs, you must bring it back to your list of priorities. There is no point in only serving others in the business world, and every act you do on behalf of your customer should be a step toward your goals. Don't be afraid to confirm that you have satisfied their needs and now it is time to show their appreciation with some business or delivering on your established and agreed-upon expectations. If you continue to give and give without any return action from your customer, are you really getting anything done? You went into business and sales to make some money and acting like UNICEF won't pay the bills. Not that there is anything wrong with UNICEF, but that type of exchange just won't cut it. Keep your goals in mind and never forget why you're there, and make sure your customer knows your purpose as well. Once you lose sight of your goal, you run the risk of becoming a sucker, and no one buys from a sucker, they only take advantage of them.

# 5

## *Talk to the Locals*

I have always been a big fan of dive bars, the kind of places that most people just walk by in favor of better lighting and more expensive drinks. Without fail, every time I walk into this type of establishment, there is at least one grizzled veteran who has a bar stool with his name on it. They have been through different owners, bartenders, and punks like me who stop through their home turf. I love talking to these guys; they always have a story about what the bar used to be like in the good old days, when a shot wasn't mixed or chilled, and when they were on top of the world. Now you can't just walk up and start a conversation with these guys; you need to establish yourself and show them that you are a quality individual before you start pumping them for information. Be wary of the local though, they're just as likely to take a swing at you, as they are to carry on a pleasant and informative conversation.

In every business organization that I have been a part of in my career, there is always a wily veteran salesperson with 30+ years in the same position. He is weathered and sometimes a little surly in his actions and statements. He has worked under countless managers, made it through mergers and layoffs. In his mind, he is the highest on the food chain, and you are just another kid who is naïve and wide-eyed. They live to tell stories about the days before the regulations and rules, when a salesperson was on an island and had to learn how to survive on his own. This type of person is an invaluable asset to you if you know what to ask them. In my experience, these colleagues are overall positive, yet skeptical of newcomers and, to some degree, new ideas. They have been around the block to know the difference between a trend and fad; they also have no time for empty strategy and talk. They have their own way of doing things, and are fairly committed to their ideas. In some cases, they will speak up

DOI: 10.4324/9781003218258-5

when no one else will, or even needs to, and while they may not always be at the top of the sales attainment chart, they are never at the bottom.

I have never been, nor do I want to be, a local. It's just not in my DNA; I like to move around an organization and try new ventures in different organizations. In some ways, I wish I did want to be a local; they have found their place in this universe and no matter how much they tell you, they love what they do for a living. During your career, you should be consistent in your self-assessment and understand what makes you happy when it comes to your actual day-to-day job, not the job description. While I doubt the locals set out to be that way, they likely found a position where they enjoyed the daily activity with a stable organization that allowed them to provide for their family without giving up their family. If you find something you love doing, strive to be a local and embrace that role. You will be a role model for the next set of great businesspeople.

A local isn't just going to hand you the keys to the kingdom. You have to show him a track record of success and, at the very least, competency and dependability. Nothing annoys a local more than someone they can't count on to get a job done. If you can't show a local this level of professionalism (or lack thereof), he will not be willing to help you. If you are good enough in a local's eye, he or she will be willing to guide you through the shark-infested waters of the business world, or at the very least provide you guidance on how to work successfully in your current organization. The locals are a wealth of knowledge and best practices; they will tell you how to get around the headaches and internal obstacles that always present themselves at the worst time. They will know a lot of your customers and have opinions about all of them. While a great deal of this information is great, most locals are a little jaded. If they tell you about a difficult customer or counterpart, make sure you still keep an open mind when dealing with these people, and always keep the local's advice in the back of your head. If you dismiss every person the local had disparaging words for, the chances are you may end up alone with the local!

Most of the time when dealing with the locals it is best to just listen and give very little input. They don't care about your anecdotes; they have them in *endless* supply and won't pay attention to yours anyway. Ask them about their mentors, the managers they enjoyed working for the most, and what they did in the past that is superior to your company's current business or sales model. I have always gotten the most out of their stories about mentors and other salespeople they thought were outstanding.

Ask them about the current team and who among them are high-caliber individuals. If they tell you someone is good, trust me they are. Please understand that your goal here is not to gossip; you are asking for their opinion and the information they share with you should remain in strict confidence. Locals don't like gossip; it shows weakness in your convictions and if you engage in this type of immature activity, you are likely to lose access to the local altogether.

The locals know how to work with customers. If they have been around for 25 or 30 years, their customers usually love them and have bought from them often. One word of caution, locals sometimes give a little too much to the customer. They will tend to bend over backward and forwards to keep the customer happy. It is important that you gain your customer's respect, but you can't let them walk all over you either. The local will know what buttons to push to get the customer to buy and know when it is time to be aggressive. I would suggest that you follow their cues until you feel it is time to change course. Customer relations is the area you can learn the most from the locals. They will understand who has the power to make the buying decision and why, along with a few extra contacts or "ins" to cut in line, ahead of your competition. The local may not hold the keys to your next promotion, but they will help you win more deals.

My favorite local is a local at the best bar in town. By this, I mean a salesperson who has been around a long time and is still a top performer. Can you imagine how talented you have to be to be a top performer at Apple or Microsoft for 20+ years? These people are worth their weight in gold, and I have been privileged enough to work with a handful of these individuals. They have been through it all and maintained a high level of success, good economies, and bad, ill-conceived strategy and product issues. You name it, they've seen it and excelled under the conditions they have found on the ground. This species of local is actually the most likely to give you time as a mentor; they enjoy helping younger professionals fine-tune their skills and will be there 24/7 to help. If I do end up a local one day, I sure as hell hope I am a local at the hot spot in town. The local is usually pretty easy to spot. When the time is right, buy him a drink and listen to the stories about selling in the era of pagers and payphones. It will be time well spent.

# 6

## Keep Your Head on a Swivel

Whenever I am out for the evening, I am constantly aware of who is around me and what their mood is at the time. I have been sucker-punched a time or two, I mean jacked in the back of the head sucker-punched. It's usually a disgruntled boyfriend or some guy who just gets mean when he drinks. In all fairness, in at least one case I probably deserved it. The business world is even more vicious in many ways and your competitors will pull every underhanded move in the book, especially if you have gotten the best of them previously. Your client will also engage in some questionable tactics based on your history or their approach to contracting and negotiations. You need to have your head on a swivel at all times, while not distracting you from your stated goals. You also need to stay close to your customers and decision-makers to let you know when the competition has started taking swings, or to be aware when you have a person within that organization that has "bad intentions."

Again, I am always conscious of what is going on around me, but my goal is not to let it take away from my good time or when it comes to work; I don't want issues that surround me to distract me from my priorities. If you are always worried about someone hitting you in the back of the head, you will never have a good time. If you get too hung up on what your competitors are doing, you stop talking about your product and show weakness. It is important to speak about your product or service 95% of the time. Please understand that we need to counter-message, that's our job, but no one wants to hear you bash your competitors. The competition is most likely a good person and if you call them a clown to your customer, you end up being the one in the circus. Being insulting or disrespectful about those selling competitive products will be the customer's negative insights into how you will handle the client when things go sideways. The

DOI: 10.4324/9781003218258-6

key is selling you and your product. You can even acknowledge that your competitor offers a quality product, but the customer needs to know why yours fits their needs better.

Before we go any further, let's address how to handle competition. It is important to remember that you don't want to "punch down," meaning if you have a better product, don't get stuck in a battle of words with a person selling an inferior product. I am not saying to ignore them, but don't let bad information get you sidetracked. If your customer gets back information from your competitor, please give them the correct information, preferably with data to back you up. No opinions, just facts. In the long run, the person giving the bad information will lose. Even if they win the first deal, you will get the next one and many more to follow.

If you are on equal or inferior footing with your product, I would deploy a strategy one of my first managers gave me: put a value on doing business with you and demonstrate this value to the customer. My manager at GE used to tell me, "There is a dollar amount associated with doing business with you and our company, make sure the customer sees it." His advice was more centered on price, and as I have advanced in my career, price is only one value to give yourself and your company. One of the most important values you can demonstrate is follow-up. I am always amazed how many businesspeople simply don't listen to what the customer is asking for and even less actually deliver on reasonable customer requests. Most of the time, we are just too focused on our goals and dismiss minor requests. Being responsive to the small things is how we win deals. I have absolutely paid more for the product if I feel the business is consistently responsive to my requests and schedule. Do the small things, they add up to big wins.

When keeping your head on a swivel, the person to worry about the most is the power drinker in the corner. You know the guy; he's got too much product in his hair, a tight shirt on, and you can just see him stewing as the night progresses. This guy will hang in the corner observing you having a good time, and this will eat at him until he blows up. The blow-up will be due to what you see as a small action, something like accidentally bumping into his buddy or having a passing conversation, or looking at his friend. This person is just looking for an excuse to cause a problem, and they can be handled in a number of ways. The most effective way is to have an ally who is in a position of authority to watch your back for you.

In the business world, this is the guy who says nothing at your presentation but makes it very clear with his facial expressions and body language that he is not buying what you are selling. This is the person who can blow up your deal behind the scenes. You will not be able to change his mind, so again, you need an ally of equal or greater influence who can be your champion. Your champion will have to step up and pump his or her chest for your product. You need to make sure you get the quiet, angry guy everything he asks for, within reason. However, if he asks for your quote, be very cautious. That information he will promptly deliver to your competitor. If he asks for it, you simply tell him that the quote has been given to the initial requestor from your quoting specialist and the information can be obtained from their colleague. This will irk Mr. Power Drinker, but you are simply following the rules that have been laid out. If Mr. Power Drinker is the one who initially requests pricing, make sure you also get it to a friend within that same organization; if not, it may get buried. Mr. Power Drinker is a tough character to deal with. In my experience, he needs to be worked around or be part of a much larger group that can overpower his negative influence.

The people you have to keep an eye on are not exclusively your customers. A member of your own party can be just as harmful to you and in many ways worse. This is the person who is willing to toss you under the bus at a moment's notice, especially if it will help their career. He will try to take advantage of the "new guy" and is the first to tell you how great he is. These people have a feeling of ultimate entitlement without any real justification. I would like to tell you that karma always gets this type of person, but it doesn't. Often, they will hang around an organization for 10 or 15 years before they are exposed as a fraud. You always want to keep them within arm's reach, but you never want to get too close to them. If you do, you will be guilty by association. The tricky part is this type of person is often super friendly and willing to help when you first meet them. These people tend to show you their true character over time. One of the most telling actions they can take is to hijack your call or deal, once you have done the work and have the deal 95% of the way done. They will tell you they are going to help you close this one, as they have done business with this customer for years and know how to get it done, outside of the established process. Once the deal closes, they will take credit for all the work you have put in and then some. There are some other key indicators that I have seen over the years; keep your eye out for these types of actions. Do they answer questions directly? These people will tend to give very few specific answers and often ignore questions altogether. Do they follow up promptly? These characters ignore questions until they work themselves out, i.e., someone does their work for them. Is their inbox a mess? If they have 1,832 unread emails and 3,287 unread text messages, I don't want them on my team. What do your customers and colleagues say about them? Be careful on this one, you don't want to gossip. Most likely people will offer the information unsolicited. You need to take a number of data points and make your own evaluation. Often, they are constantly complaining and blaming others for their situation. So be wary of the guy in your own party who is looking to start trouble.

To quote *Back to School*, one of my favorite movies, "It's tough out there, you have to look out for number one and make sure you don't step in number two." You have to keep your head on a swivel but focus on what you do well and not on what your competitor is trying to do to you. The more you focus on you and only retaliate when it is necessary, the better off you will be in the long run.

# 7

## If You Don't Have a "Big" Friend, Make One

I am not a fighter, and although I have had a few issues with some characters over the years, I usually make it through my evenings unscathed. I have to think that is due to the fact I don't ask for it and probably even more importantly, I have always had "big" friends who weren't to be messed with. My two best friends from high school played big-time college lacrosse and football; my two best friends from college are 6'8" and started as a freshman on our basketball team and a scrappy 6'3" kid from Philly. With friends like these, I could pretty much do whatever I wanted to do, and no one would fool with me. They also had my back through thick and thin, and I never, ever questioned their loyalty. I am confident that they could say the same thing about me. These are friends who I am still close with today; they were all at my wedding and we all have children of similar ages.

You need "big" friends in the business world, or you will be in constant danger. In the business community, the big friends are those people you work with who can be trusted with privileged information and are always looking out for your best interest. They offer unsolicited advice when you may not want to hear it, but they truly care about your wellbeing. I can say that of all the resources you have access to, "big friends" in the corporate world are the most valuable. The best ones are usually manager level and above and are not about "me" they are about "we." They will never hold you back from advancing your career and are confident enough to not have to worry about kissing someone else's backside and don't require a bunch of brown nosers around them. They respect and trust you unless you give them a reason not to. Big friends also tend to have some, if not significant, influence in your organization, because quite simply they have earned it!

DOI: 10.4324/9781003218258-7

I can count my true friends on one hand, and I have about as many people whom I rely on in my professional life. Just like having a "big" friend, having a true business friend is someone who has earned your trust and he feels the same way about you. A warning, you need to exercise extreme caution when trusting a colleague with sensitive information. Quite frankly, I never disclose personal or sensitive information with anyone, until they have demonstrated an ability to keep information to themselves. I have seen far too many people fall into the telephone game. They give a juicy detail to someone who is always looking to hear something new, and the next thing you know what was once a secret is common knowledge. You need to start small. If you feel you have met someone at work who is *trustworthy*, you can float a fairly inconsequential piece of information about a customer. If it makes its way back to you, that person is a gossip hound, not a friend. The true "big friends" are a vault, and they are highly likely to be very protective of their information as well. Choose your friends wisely in the business world. If you don't, you can open yourself up to embarrassment or allow someone to take advantage of you.

I have been lucky enough to have some managers I considered "big" friends, but this is certainly the exception and not the rule. Just because someone is your manager doesn't mean they will have your back. This should not be the case, but unfortunately some people have one goal and one goal only, self-promotion. This is the guy who talks a big game, but when it hits the fan, he slips into the background or hides under the table. Chances are, they have climbed to their "leadership" position, by getting close to another weak leader. They are simply corporate climbers, people who know how to excel in an environment where it is more important to have a connection than actually be a productive leader. A true manager or supervisor will fight for his people while putting them in a position that best suits them, allowing their team to be successful. He will always be on your side during an internal battle, because as a true friend, you will never put him in a position where they have to lie or cheat for you.

I always hear, "My boss threw me under the bus." Well, of course he did if you put him in a position that if he covered for you, he would have destroyed his credibility because you were in the wrong. This relationship is a two-way street. No one wants a friend who expects the world but is never there when help is needed. Make sure you are a good faith partner with your management. If you are a reliable employee, your boss will stretch and ask for special treatment for you when you really need it. If you are constantly asking for help or asking them to make exceptions for you, there will be no equity left when you really need it. You have to earn this friendship, a true leader will not let anyone take advantage of them, even their own employee.

Having "big" friends does not give you free range to be a jackass. You have to continue to foster your relationship and ensure you don't take them for granted. If you get too big for your britches and continue to make your friends cover your butt, you will wear that relationship so thin it will disappear. I have seen this too many times. Someone continues to pick fights at the bar and the "big" friend bails them out one too many times. One day you will talk to the wrong person at the wrong time and your "big" friend will get sick of bailing you out and let you get knocked out. Then you will be bruised, bloodied, and down one friend, which will cost you dearly down the road. Having "big" friends is great; just make sure you don't abuse them.

This correlates very easily to the business world. If you are fortunate enough to be working under a true leader, yet you continue to screw up and need someone to cover for you constantly, you will wear that leader down to a point where they not only won't help you, they will actually cut you off completely. Again, this relationship has to be a two-way street to be sustainable. The best way to keep your boss on your side is to deliver and always be responsive. Don't cut corners on your projects, expecting him or her to cover for your shortcomings. When you see an opportunity to help or perhaps make their life easier, do it and don't expect anything in return. A good deed doesn't carry much weight if you are expecting something in return. Be an example for your manager, not a kiss ass. If you do things the right way, you will be rewarded first with success (which should be your main goal here), and second with loyalty from your new "big" friend.

Unfortunately, you will likely work for people who are the exact opposite of your friend. Their only priority is themselves and they will only do things that are easy for them if they benefit you. They will reserve their political capital for the items that most benefit them and if you gain some secondary reward, so be it. Other telltale signs of this type of person are a lack of follow-up, little value creation for you, and a willingness to ditch you and your team when the executives come around. They also tend to take credit for work they did not do. It is important to be productive for this type of manager but keep them at arm's length. However, before you accuse your manager of this type of behavior, make sure you haven't abused their loyalty. So don't point fingers until you are 100% sure your house is in order.

There is also one more anecdote when it comes to making "big" friends. If you are dealing with someone from the military, especially if he went to one of the service academies, they are most likely trustworthy. I did not attend one of these institutions, nor did I serve my country in the military, but my best friend has, and I have hired or helped many of his colleagues get hired when they have transitioned to the civilian world. In my experience, I am 100% confident in people from this background. If I have two candidates of similar ability, I will always hire someone with a military background. The military teaches discipline and loyalty, two things I need from my employees and colleagues. They are always open to training and feedback, and know how to push through adversity. If you have a "big" friend who is also from the military, you are riding high in life and career.

# 8

## Respect the Bouncers

As you can probably tell by now, I have been in a number of bars in my life. Some were very high-end: $1,000-bottle-type places; some cleaned teeth up at the end of the night. No matter what type of place it was, there was always a set of rules that had to be followed, and bouncers are the ones who enforced those rules. The bouncers are unique decision-makers in the bar; they decide who stays and who goes. Some bouncers' rules were very restrictive in nature; some were barely visible. Basically, don't steal anything out of the register and you were okay. Regardless of their philosophy on managing the bar rules, if you crossed the line, they all would come down with a vengeance. Many of them actually enjoyed the process of giving someone the boot!

In the business world, there are also varying sets of rules. You need to recognize what they are and follow them to the letter. Some of your customers will have very structured decision-making processes, and others will be so unorganized and free-flowing that it will be difficult to figure out who is making the decision. Either way, it is incumbent on you to figure out the rules of the game and watch the "bouncers" to see if you are staying in line. Whatever the rules are, make sure you stay within reasonable boundaries, many of the business bouncers will also take pleasure in giving your deal to your biggest competitor, often to simply make the point that they are in charge, not you.

Whether you have a private party or are just part of the crowd, you can always be kicked out of any bar. I have seen it happen far too often in deals where a certain vendor is in the catbird seat, gets overconfident, and begins to push the rules of the game. This will invariably end up in a lost deal for a person who if they just would've stayed within the boundaries, would have won the deal, instead they walk away with a loss. Just like in the bar, the

DOI: 10.4324/9781003218258-8

bouncers in the business world will give you leeway to some degree. If they know you and have had good experiences with you in the past, you will be given a large margin for error. However, this type of equity can be spent very quickly if you act like you are above the law. Once you step over the line, you will be escorted out of the deal very quickly. If you step way over the line, you will be tossed out on your butt and told to never return again.

The customer will most likely lay out a set of rules for you to follow. For example, they will have all quotes go to one person, have presentations for an hour from each potential vendor, and set the timeline for a decision. These rules are non-negotiable, no matter how much equity you build up. If you ignore the defined guidelines, you will not win the deal. It should be a simple thing to accomplish, but either negligence, lack of knowing what these rules are, or incompetence from an individual or organization will lead to the ball being dropped. If you don't know what the rules of the game are, you need to ask. Don't make assumptions about the non-negotiable rules. If you are not sure, ask someone you trust on the inside. The fact that many of your competitors either don't know or won't ask what the rules of the deal are will benefit you at times, assuming you stay within the boundaries set by the customer.

The hard part of dealing with bouncers is trying to figure out the unwritten rules of the game. I have been escorted out of bars when I felt I did very little to deserve it, seriously very little. I have also been kicked out of bars when I absolutely deserved it. Deals are the same way. I have won on price, won on quality of product, and had decision-makers in my court and still lost deals. Most of the time in these situations I lost because there were agreements struck on a national or top executive level. I didn't have the unwritten rules of the game, and someone outside of the normal decision-making structure was driving the decision. For a smaller percentage of time, another vendor set the rules and my customer was their puppet. This is a role that I have been in before, but usually I am the one playing the puppet master. When you are facing this type of scenario, your customer will know every weakness you have, some real and some perceived. They have bought into the competitor's story or have just been bought by the competitor, and with every day that passes, your competition will provide more fuel to this fire. Either way, the bouncer will be waiting to trip you up. And as soon as this happens, you guessed it, "Please sir, let me escort you outside." Nighty-night, bon voyage, all of your time and efforts have been wasted.

Let me set the scene. A vendor is a true partner with a customer. The customer gives the vendor 80–100% of their business and things are moving along nicely for both. After a few years, the attention this customer once saw from the vendor starts to be given to new customers and new initiatives. Soon, the customer feels they are being taken for granted. The vendor senses this and picks up the pace again for this customer for a relatively short period of time. Soon the vendor falls back into old habits and more mistakes are made. Next there is an issue with the product or service. Then, one day the vendor receives a request from the customer (if he is lucky), stating that they are opening the next bid to a group of vendors "to see what else is out there." This is ugly and a big, big problem. This vendor has lost this customer and will bring in the big guns to try and save it. The CEO, COO, and managers will come in and talk about the good old days and how changing vendors will hurt their supply chain and cause headaches for the organization. In my experience, once you get to this point with your customer, it is very difficult to keep them, and the relationship has forever been changed for all parties involved.

The problem with this strategy is that the vendor has been causing the headaches for a while now and the good old days are long gone. More times than not, they will see the business dwindle over time. This vendor has been kicked out of a private party, and this type of loss will sting for years. Once you are a partner to a customer, you have to manage their expectations. You will have to go out and get new business, but you also have to stay in regular contact with the customer. With big success comes big responsibility and monthly or quarterly reviews are a must with your true partners. You have to give direction for the future and give the impression that they are special and even though you will have new customers, they are still a priority. You will have a lot of leeway with this type of customer, but as the saying goes, "Trust is the hardest thing to gain and the easiest thing to lose." Don't take your private party for granted; you are never above the law, never. It is a simple rule, and a cliché for a reason, treat others how you want to be treated. If you have a discount for new customers or your CEO is taking a roadshow, make sure you include your best customers. Don't waste all of your enticing extras on new customers while letting the clients who have paid your bills for the last few years stand pat. Bring in coffee or lunch for no apparent reason at all—"I want to do this because you are important to me and my business, I thank you for your loyalty!" These small gestures will go a long way toward maintaining your best clients for years to come.

You have to respect the bouncers and their rules in any situation. If you don't, you will be on the outside looking in for a long time. Even if you make it back in another night, the bouncers will remember you and be watching you closely. What used to be a comfortable environment will turn into a place where you feel you are constantly being watched and even the smallest mistake will lead to bad outcomes. For most of us, following the rules is boring. It is much more fun to push the envelope and see what we can do outside of the guardrails provided by the customer. If you push, do so with an awareness that violating the "bouncers'" rules can lead to undesirable results.

# 9

## Drink Responsibly

I read a book called *The Oz Principle* early in my professional life; my main takeaway was the importance of attitude and accountability in the corporate world. The book influenced me more than any other book I had read to that point in life and left me with one thing I always try to remember: your scope of responsibility is boundless. Have you ever seen someone who is getting ready to be bounced from the bar? In my experience, they always find someone else to blame for their actions, and they always claim there is some sort of misunderstanding. I have never seen someone get kicked out of a bar and take it well, but at the end of the day, the person getting the boot is responsible for their forced exit from the pub.

When I say your scope of responsibility is boundless, I mean that no matter whether you dropped the ball or not, if something goes wrong with your customer it is always your fault. A customer may tell you they understand, and that this doesn't really fall under your job title, and they don't blame you, but at the end of the day, they are looking to you for a solution. If the shipping company loses the package, it's your job to find it. If the system goes down and production stops, you need to fix it. You didn't properly set expectations and your customer didn't receive the value they expected, that's definitely on you.

This is a cruel fact of business and sales, and it is often a difficult pill to swallow. But swallow it you must, and the more insight you have into every aspect of your deal, the better off you will be in the long run. Take all necessary steps to ensure that there will be no breakdown within the structure of your deal. The important thing to remember is that you can only control your controllables. You can control price, customer expectations, and your availability; this is where your focus must remain.

DOI: 10.4324/9781003218258-9

However, you need to make sure your organization is set up to properly support you and plan accordingly if you have areas of weakness.

Let me give you an example. Your customer committed to a sale, so the hard work is done, right? You have beaten all of the competitors, and the customer has bought into your message and product. Your product requires substantial construction and site preparation. Your organization has a process in which your construction team is notified along with some sort of project manager. Most salespeople I know will get the sale, start the process, and move onto the next deal. The celebration time for a win is brief and your sales quota requires you to move on. However, I can say with all certainty that your deal is not done! You need to establish a rapport with all members of the team who will be involved. Even though you can't install the product and you aren't the project manager, there has to be communication between the parties, and you have to stay in contact with the customer until the job is completely done. I have had a number of customers tell me that one of their vendors sold them a product or service and they never saw them again. This is a recipe for disaster and will certainly lead to trouble for the vendor the next time the customer is in the market to buy. In short, your deal is not done when the contract is signed. In fact, your deal is never really done; your initial win is an extended "interview" for your next opportunity.

Another more common example of this is when you are working on closing a deal with your customer and the deal hits a snag or is squashed by a decision-maker you haven't been working with up until that point. Let's be clear, this is 100% your fault. This equates to you going into a pub and ordering a drink from the busboy. You have got a commitment from a person who has essentially no power in the final decision-making process. I am not saying that you ignore everyone but the final decision-maker; their approval is often required to close the deal. However, you have to know who cuts the PO, who is the person signing on the dotted line and ultimately responsible for the purchase. You must understand the internal processes of your customer. If you make the assumption that winning at a lower level of the organization will automatically influence executives within that organization, you are sorely mistaken. You have to bring something to the decision-maker's table. At the very least, you need to have a strong internal advocate to take your message to leadership. Ideally, you should have both. You need to have insight into these details, or you will lose deals that should have been won. When you are in the midst of a competitive deal, an honest and frank evaluation of your position must take place. Do you know who is the final decision-maker? What is your relationship with them? Are you confident that the final decision-maker will advocate for your product? If any of these answers are no, or I am not sure, you have more work to do, or your other champion better be willing to fight to the end for your product. If not, your chances of winning are extremely low.

Also, under this subject, never blame someone within your organization for a mistake that was made, even if it was their fault. You are a salesperson; you have to be able to spin a mistake and make your customer feel that they are important, so important that you pulled a number of strings to take care of the problem. Any salesperson who says, "That is Rob Smith's job. You should call him, and he will take care of it," has instantly lost credibility with that customer. Doesn't this sound better? "My team will take care of this; I will get a resolution for you as soon as possible. I'm sorry for the inconvenience." I call it playing politician. A good politician will rarely, if ever, denigrate a member of their own party. A good politician will rarely even blame a member of the other party. They will present a solution to the problem, and the voter will realize that someone else caused the problem. It is not a hard and fast rule, but politicians who solve problems are re-elected; salespeople who solve problems win deals. You can blame others and win some deals, especially if you have a superior product. However, if you are evenly matched blaming others will lead to losses down the road. Either way, not taking responsibility will have a significant negative impact on your credibility.

I know this sounds simple and you would tell me you've never done anything like this in your career, but if you take an honest look at yourself, it is my guess that you have pushed responsibility onto someone else when you could have and should have taken care of the issue. I suspect that you may have lost a follow-up deal with that customer or at the very least you didn't have a strong partnership with them while they were your customer.

The last example is the situation that bothers me the most. Imagine five people standing in a room with a product that is mutually beneficial to them all and is functioning improperly. The five people go back and forth with each other about whose responsibility this is for neglecting to take any action on the broken unit. They continue this back and forth for several hours and finally come to the conclusion that they have to go back to their individual divisions to see what actions they can take, agreeing to meet again tomorrow. In the meanwhile, the product is still broken, and your customer is still in need of a solution. You will ask them for patience as a solution is found, forcing the customer to wait longer than necessary. I have seen this more times than I care to remember, and I find that I am the one who usually takes the action to fix the problem. Many times, I have heard, "I apologize for the inconvenience, and I am waiting for my team to find a solution." Wrong answer. You sold it. You need to figure out a way to get it fixed. Your customer knows that you don't have the skill set to fix it, but they certainly expect you to find the person who does. Provide the customer daily status updates, hold your colleagues to account, and don't worry about stepping on a few toes! In short, when an issue arises make sure you are available and transparent on timelines for your customer. Do not tell them the fix will take hours when you are sure it will take days. Also, do not "ghost" your client. Part of that commission you received as part of closing the deal is taking the tough phone call about issues with your product. You will be amazed how your customer will react to just hearing their frustrations. When you receive this call, make sure you listen, empathize, and commit to following up on a daily basis, until the issue is resolved.

I have worked in complex, multi-functional organizations, and there are always people who don't want to do their job. It is incumbent upon you to get them to perform by any means necessary. First, you have to be certain that this individual is truly the one to fix the problem. Once that is clear, you need to have a respectful and frank discussion about the issue, the plan to fix it, and the timeline. This will allow you to communicate specifics to your customer. The "Bob is going to fix it; he'll give you a call" is not enough. You need to give specific action items and reasonable timelines to the customer, or they will make up their own. If you can't get this counterpart motivated to commit to this project, you have to take it up the chain of command. I'm not saying call their VP, but at least have you or someone higher in your food chain communicate with their management. That being said, it is always better to handle this situation yourself. I only involve my boss if his help is absolutely necessary.

I have been guilty of not escalating these types of issues in the past and I have always paid dearly for it. You have to be upfront and honest if someone is not doing his job; if he takes offense to it, he won't be around for long anyway. However, you better make sure that you have done everything in your power before you call someone else out. If you didn't take an action to fix the problem that you could have, you have no right to call someone else on the carpet. At the end of the day, you have business relationships with the people you work with, you are not there to make friends.

Please don't be the "it's not my job" salesperson. You give us all a bad name while making yourself look foolish and immature no matter your age. Be a problem solver and look at these issues as an opportunity to shine in the eyes of your customer.

This is important. If you are concerned about your company's culture of accountability, run away as fast as you can. If you don't, your ability to solve problems will be eliminated and going to work every day will be unbearable.

# 10

## *Bar Stool Selling*

One of my favorite things to do is to get a couple of stools at the local watering hole and hang out with my family and friends; it was something I missed so much as COVID-19 took hold of the world. It is such a unique environment, one where you don't have to worry about cooking food or preparing food for your guests, so it gives you the opportunity to have full conversations (as long as you can keep your face out of your phone). There have been a number of important decisions in my life that took place in this type of setting. My wife and I will often go out for a date and grab a seat at the bar while waiting for a table. We will discuss our family, friends, finances, politics—you name it. It is one of the only public settings where people will divulge personal information in the hopes of gleaning some sort of insight from someone else. I am sure you have had similar conversations and they were just that, conversations. There wasn't an opening, a body, a probing question, and then a close. You asked appropriate questions, you shut your mouth when it was the proper time, and you spoke passionately about something. The purpose of your discussion was to learn, not to get someone to buy something from you or discuss the technical details of the cocktail in your hand. You speak to people in the pub setting because you want to find out what they think and how they work as a human.

A colleague of mine in 2005 got the idea of the Bar Stool Selling in my head. He is a very successful salesperson and he once said to me, "I try to sell like I am talking to my customer over a drink at the bar." It just clicked in my head and as I sold more and socialized more, I kept seeing the parallels between the bar scene and the business world. His philosophy is something I continue to keep in mind when making and preparing for sales calls. My best sales calls and presentations have been the ones that didn't feel like a sales call. We discussed and debated with passion and

DOI: 10.4324/9781003218258-10

deliberation. There was definitely a goal laid out and accomplished, but I never had to push it on the customer. I listened more than I spoke, but when I spoke, it was impactful and helpful to the customer. Remember that part, listen more than you speak. There is a reason you have two ears and one mouth.

Have you ever had a conversation with someone who constantly talked over you and never asked you a question, so you had to offer up or even force your point of view into the conversation? Even when you did get to complete your thought, the person barely acknowledged your point and started in on when they found themselves in a similar situation and shared their experience. My guess is you did not enjoy it and gave up to let him talk some more, or you found another person to converse with as soon as possible. That is the way most of my sales calls were when I started selling. It was basically verbal diarrhea, never yielding stellar results. Yes, I did win deals, but not as much as I could have. The minute I learned to shut up and listen, I mean really listen, selling became exponentially easier.

Listening is the key to crafting a message that serves both you and your customers' interests. It will also allow you to uncover new opportunities that will lead to more sales. Listening is something you must make an effort to do well; it is not just keeping quiet, waiting for your turn to talk. It is hearing the message that the customer is giving to you, digesting it, and responding directly to their request. If you listen properly, the customer will unveil their personality, goals, and fears, but you must make an effort to truly hear what the client is telling you. There are a few things to watch out for to understand if your goals align with what your customer is telling you they need. Do they stick to the agenda that was laid out? Are they asking very detail-oriented questions? Do they allow themselves to get off on different tangents or are they non-committal and friendly? You want to mirror the personality with whom you are speaking. If the customer is direct and to the point, they likely want you to be concise and to the point. If they are detailed oriented, they want you to dig into the guts of your product or service and really allow them to pick it apart. Go off on their tangents with them but find a way to bring it back to your agenda. If they are non-committal, don't give them the full court press and try to close hard right out of the gate. I have found that patience is synonymous with listening. Most businesspeople want to rush to meet their goals, often steamrolling over their target audience. You have to be patient enough to address your customer's reasonable needs, prior to pushing your agenda.

I have rarely had a conversation with a friend or family member in which I didn't ask a laundry list of questions. However, I have neglected to do this on my sales calls, and I have missed opportunities because of this practice. Questions are extremely important in the selling process, but they can also shut down a presentation if they are "canned" sales questions. Most of my questions are simple, "What do you need from me?" or "What needs are you looking to fill?" These will open more doors than you can imagine. A question like, "If there was a product that could reduce cost and increase productivity, would you be interested in it?" will not get you anywhere. Of course they are interested; that's like asking if you would be interested in a 70-inch HD television that was also a free ATM and makes world-class steaks. "Uh yeah, I'm interested in that." But you haven't learned anything about what my expectations are of you and what my needs are for my company. This really isn't that hard. Do you have to search for a question to ask when you are drinking with your buddies? No, because you have set the agenda and most importantly you asked them the appropriate question, "What do you want to drink?" not "Do you want a drink?" One forces a conversation, the other forces a follow-up question, unless of course they say "no." Don't give your client the chance to say "no" by asking them a closed-ended question.

Speaking with passion is also extremely important when selling. When you and a friend are discussing a topic, you both have opinions and try to give strong reasons on why your opinion is the right one. Your discussions don't end in fistfights, but they are passionate. It is important to be passionate about your product or service, but not emotional. People often use these words interchangeably, but they could not be more wrong. Behind passion there is reason and logic, behind emotion there is ignorance. A passionate salesperson gives compelling reasons to buy his product and shows his self-confidence in a quiet and strong way. An emotional salesperson bashes his competition and tries to cover their insecurities with arrogance. It is important to know the difference between passion and emotion and be sure you check emotion at the door. Emotion almost always leads to bad outcomes, whether you are in the bar or in the board room.

You don't have to be heartless; I would argue that if you are passionate, you will demonstrate more empathy in one sales call than an emotional salesperson will show in a month. With passion also comes respect for others and their opinions. Emotion is usually accompanied by closed-mindedness and disrespect. You have to respect other opinions when you are selling to them. When you are trying to displace the incumbent vendor, you are essentially telling a customer that what they are doing is wrong and you have the right solution. If you are not respectful when selling to your customer, you will never sell them anything. I ask you to watch the top performers in your company sell and I guarantee you will see their passion. You will hear his conviction and he will not accept anything that disparages his product, but he is still respectful toward the customer. This top performing is never dismissive of the client's opinion, and they also never miss the chance to counter-message in a respectful and informative way.

Part of selling is also being able to read the non-verbal signs your customer gives you. Then you must react accordingly. For those of you who are single, you do the same thing when you are speaking to someone who you are interested in dating. Is he or she making eye contact? Is he or she making a point to touch you? Is he or she looking over your shoulder to see who she can talk to next? Unless you are receiving positive non-verbal signals, you are likely not going down a positive path.

With your customers you have to pay attention and react to their body language as well. Sometimes these signs are subtle: a softening of their brow or leaning into your discussion are good signs. If they start to shuffle papers, look at the phone, or cross their arms you may be in trouble. I could give a list of signs, but if you are paying attention, you can tell if the body language is giving you the green or red light. If you are receiving negative non-verbal signals, it doesn't mean you are sunk, you simply need to change course to match your customer's style. Constant evaluation is needed, think about if you interrupted your client or if you did not completely address their question or issue. If your enthusiasm is not being matched by your customer's reserved approach, sit back in your seat, lower your tone, and speak slower. Read the room and react to the conditions you see.

It is important to remember that you can sell and have a conversation at the same time. By that I mean, you can sell your product and still interact as if you were speaking to a friend at the bar. The Bar Stool selling approach is more a state of mind than a process, the key is being aware of your words and actions along with your customer's words and actions. You need to be comfortable in your own skin and confident in your value to put this theory into action. Please keep in mind, I said confident, not arrogant. If you are confident, passionate, and not emotional, you will earn the trust and confidence of your customer, leading to more business and bigger paychecks. More money won't solve all of your problems, but it will certainly take an issue off the table and make your work enjoyable.

# 11

## You're Going to Get Shot Down, Deal with It

Regardless of your current relationship status, there has been a time at some point in your bar life when you have attempted to speak to an attractive person at the bar and have been shot down. I can say from personal experience, sometimes it is in spectacular fashion and to the amusement of your friends. You had two choices: either take it like an adult or lash out at the individual who blew you off and make yourself look like a fool. While it seems quite evident what the correct choice is, it should be no surprise that people take the incorrect path quite often in this scenario. When I first started selling, I really had a difficult time getting shot down or, based on my personality, blown off. I could always deal with getting shot down, but being ignored or minimized was something I really struggled with at the beginning of my career. The tough part is that the less experience you have the more you get shot down, and the tougher it is to deal with. It is truly a Catch-22, you're learning how to do your job, but until you are good at it, many of your top prospects won't give you the time of day. It is critical to develop a thick skin early on in this game and learn how to power through negativity from your customers. You have to learn how to deal with rejection, without ever accepting it.

The old expression is, "Never take no for an answer." I used to really get annoyed with clichés, but they exist for a reason, and you should not ignore them. If your customer tells you no, you haven't done a good job selling, full stop. Once you are told no, you need to start selling again while changing your strategy and approach. Make sure the customer is clear on the benefits of your product and the value you bring. Regardless of your

DOI: 10.4324/9781003218258-11

strategy or execution, there will be many times in your career when you will lose deals. You simply can't win them all, but again, you don't have to be satisfied with a loss.

If the customer has decided to go with a different vendor or service, the worst thing you can do is be *belligerent*. How many times has a temper tantrum netted you anything as an adult? No one will buy something from you in the future if you act like a jerk when someone else won the business that you wanted. Resist the urge to tell a customer how bad a decision they have made, and they will live to regret it. Whether it was in sports or business, I have always used my losses as motivation, not as an impediment. As soon as you have lost, you have to begin to position yourself as the vendor they will come back to when they are out shopping again. You have to be next in line once you have lost. Working with the mentality that you will show the customer how wrong they were is fine, just make sure that isn't verbalized to the client, other clients, or your colleagues. Check emotion at the door and remember that passion is good, emotion makes you do stupid things that you will never recover from.

After a rejection, you have to be willing to refocus, change course, and come back again in order to break down the customer's barrier. There will be people who turn you down just because you are a salesperson. The key to this is not to keep coming back and being used for a punching bag. No one will respect someone who keeps coming back to be abused, you have to keep pushing with real product benefits and respectful counterpoints. Keep it professional and don't hold grudges if someone takes their business elsewhere. You can hold all of the grudges you want; it won't affect your customer one bit. Remember they chose a different product, and your vendetta will not affect them in the slightest. There aren't too many products out there that have customers falling all over themselves to buy. And even if you had one of those products, if you tried to play the payback game with a certain customer, you still would lose in the long run. The customer will find every excuse to not buy from you, even if your product is better and cheaper, they will punish themselves with inferior products to spite you. The rejections that come into your life will become what build your strength and character as a salesperson. Every time I have lost a deal, my response to the customer has always been to wish them luck and to have them let me know if there is anything I can do to help in the future. Staying positive after getting shot down is a challenge, also a requirement to be successful in this world.

There are many ways to deal with rejection; some people try to separate themselves from it and walk away for a while; others want to break down everything that may have gone wrong and step up the heat on themselves. I have found that accepting the loss honorably and walking away is best for all parties. When I say walk away, I am not talking about a year. You need to give the customer some time to install the new product or iron out the kinks in the new system. Once enough time has passed, go visit that customer to see your competitor's product in action. It is perfectly acceptable to appreciate and compliment another product. Chances are the competition will drop the ball and your willingness to show your face in front of a customer that has shot you down will show your professionalism and maturity. Trust me, if it is a complete disaster, they will call you.

What you don't want to do is be there, staring over their shoulder, pointing out all of the things that are going wrong with the new product. The customer has put their reputation on the line by buying this product, and they will not be willing to admit they are wrong very easily or quickly. It would be like confronting your ex-girlfriend and her new boyfriend to tell her what is wrong with her new man. How do you think you would come off in that type of scenario? If it isn't obvious, you come off as desperate and I promise you will not win back that girl or that customer. You are better off showing the customer who has left you what you do so well. Most likely they will still call you from time to time if the other vendor is short on the product or they don't carry something you do. Make sure your service on this type of call is impeccable. Ask them how their business is going and tell them about your new offerings and how well things are going in your world. Also be sure to tell them you are looking forward to another shot at their business in the future and be specific on things that you see as possible future projects. Nothing is harder or more satisfying than getting a client back who went to another competitor last time around. That type of win warms my soul and gets me through any tough selling situations.

Another strategy is to use the powerful tool of *self-deprivation*. Being willing to admit that you are not perfect and make light of yourself or your company does a number of things to position you for the next deal. Even if you don't think you messed up, your customer does, or they would have bought from you. Bring up the shortcomings of the last sales process, and when you sell next time around, don't make the same perceived mistakes. It is also beneficial to admit your organization is not perfect;

this will actually give you some cushion to make small mistakes. If you promise perfection, you better deliver, and perfection rarely happens. If your price was too high, talk to your customer about your bosses being a little removed from reality on the last deal. This does two things: first, it admits a mistake, and second, it tells the customer, "I am trying to be on your side here and next time my approach will be better." A little self-deprecation can go a long way in the bar or the boardroom.

I'd like to share some advice my grandfather gave me (God rest his soul). "Suck it up, rub some dirt on it and walk it off. This game is for big boys/girls, if you want to cry you can go back and play with the little kids." This advice left me with bloody noses, lips, and countless other bumps and bruises. It also made me tough and taught me the best thing to do when you lose is to come back next time more prepared and stronger. Your customer doesn't care about your delicate feelings, just like the person at the bar who shot you down. When the client is buying, they do so with their own self-interest in mind. No matter how nice of a person you are, and how big of a jerk your competition is, if they outwork and outsell you, the jerk will win. Put on your big kid pants and do better next time.

On the other side of the coin, don't be the businessperson that wins and gloats. As previously stated, one of the biggest turn-offs for your clients is when you bash the competition. Even worse is when you "kick dirt on the grave" of a competitor that you just beat out. Few, if any, clients respond to bullies; think of it as business sportsmanship. One of the key lessons they teach you in golf is being gracious in defeat *and* victory. After a win on the field, did we shake hands and say, "You guys stink, I don't know why you came out"? Of course not. Learning how to win the right way is as important, if not more so, than how to lose the right way. Don't be a sore winner.

In my career, I have been surrounded by a number of individuals who were more talented, but I have yet to be outworked. I believe the ability to come back from being shot down is all about your attitude and willingness to work. If you have a positive attitude and a work ethic, you will, at the very least, allow yourself to be successful. I am not saying you always have to be Mr. or Ms. Sunshine. We all need to vent from time to time, but you can't let it affect your day-to-day activity. This game is not an easy one, and you must embrace the difficulty of winning business. Some of you may recognize this quote: "The hard is what makes it great; if it was easy, everyone would do it." This applies to many facets of life; nothing in life worth working for is easy. If you had customers falling all over themselves to buy your product or service, you wouldn't be needed. The challenges we face in the business world are job security and when working under difficult circumstances, we are bound to fail from time to time. Your attitude and work ethic will carry you through the tough times, and keep you motivated to keep fighting for the next win, or maybe even the next loss. No one wins all the time; if you can find it in yourself to persevere through the losses, success will soon follow.

# 12

## *Be the Center of Attention, to a Point*

Have you ever seen a very attractive person with a decent but fairly average-looking member of the opposite sex? In my younger years, I always wondered why so many attractive women would settle for an average Joe. Then it finally hit me: this average Joe had charisma. This word is thrown around often, but what it really means to me is the ability to be so compelling that others want to be around you and follow you. In order to be charismatic, you must be comfortable in your own skin; you must truly enjoy your surroundings, and you must find your way to the center of attention in most environments. Notice I said find your way to the center of attention, not force yourself to the center of attention. If you have to force it you are not being charismatic, you are being obnoxious. The first thing you have to remember is the center of attention is where you are, not where someone else is. You must know how to carry the crowd and have enough substance to justify the attention that you are being given. Most importantly, you must know when to fade into the background.

You may be saying that's great when I'm out having a drink, but what does this have to do with sales? Good question. In order to be the center of attention in the sales world, you need to create interest from your customers by highlighting the benefits of your product or service. It is easy to sell to a customer who needs your product; that is like being the center of attention at your birthday party. The difficult task is getting the customer excited about a product they don't think they need to understand how it applies to their everyday operations. In essence, it is getting a person excited about someone else's birthday.

When I think of selling in competitive or new markets, I think about attending a wedding. I love weddings; I have been at weddings and received invitations to the weddings of people I just met that evening. I am in my

DOI: 10.4324/9781003218258-12

element at weddings because I know my role. I am there to be part of the festivities and be the life of the party without taking away from the truly important people that evening, the bride and groom. Weddings are very similar to a competitive market. You have a number of suitors all trying to accomplish the same goal. At a wedding, the suitors are looking to have fun. In the business world, the suitors are looking to win business. There is always the guy who starts out strong; he is out dancing early, buying drinks at the bar, and usually in bed by 9 pm. There is the "look at me" guy, the guy doing the worm in the middle of the circle, but as soon as you try to talk to him, all he has to say is, "YMCA"! In my experience, it is better to stay in your lane and not force your way into the center of attention, let it come to you.

I love weddings because they allow you to interact with a number of people with different backgrounds, ages, and perspectives. I always enjoy weddings because I find touchpoints with as many people as I can without being overbearing and obnoxious. I try to do the same thing when I am selling: find touchpoints with as many decision-makers as possible and try to find a connection with them along the way. For that matter, I like to contact as many people as possible in the organization when trying to secure business. Whether they technically are a decision-maker or not, you can never be sure who's opinion will be considered when evaluating products and vendors. It is always good policy to sell to everyone in an attempt to get them excited about your products and how they can potentially improve their everyday operations.

It is great to be the center of attention, but you also need to know when to fade into the background. To revert to weddings, you could be a rockstar at the wedding; I'm talking a Vince Vaughn in *Wedding Crashers* performance. But nobody wants you cutting the cake for them; you need to know when your work is done and when you need to become a wallflower. In the course of winning a deal, you will have to be front and center often, but one of the hardest things to do is walk away for a week or so while the customer is going through their internal process. You need to be aware of the steps and have a reasonable expectation of when the customer will get back to you, but you can't force your way into the behind-closed-door meetings very often. You have to rest on the fact that you have done everything you can, and it is no longer your party. Be the center of attention until it is time to fade into the background. If you keep your eyes and ears open, it will be very clear when this is the case. When the time comes to come back to the party, your people on the inside will let you know.

I have hung out with a number of people who were great company, once. The second time around opened my eyes to the fact that they weren't cool; they were obnoxious, and I really didn't want anything to do with them. You will see this from time to time, where a salesperson who is over the top with his sales technique and hyperbole will win one deal. When the second deal comes around, he uses the exact same approach, and the customer sees right through him. He is essentially a one-trick pony. It is important to show versatility in the business world, while relying on your strengths. It gets back to what we discussed about adapting to your environment and reaching out of your comfort zone. I do not want you to abandon what has made you successful, I am asking you to build on your strengths. Think of an acquaintance who tells the same jokes and stories that were funny the first time and kind of pathetic the second time. You can imagine him telling the same jokes and stories in every crowd of people he meets. Some customers may be wowed by aggressive promises and fireworks come deal closing time. The problem with this type of over-the-top action for every deal is it becomes obnoxious to the customer.

There is a very clear line between being charismatic and being obnoxious. Obnoxious people aren't comfortable in their own skin, and even though they might get a deal from time to time due to their actions, they have no real staying power. Charisma is born from self-confidence; being obnoxious comes from insecurity. If you truly are the center of attention because you have charisma your customers and coworkers will trust you as a peer, resulting in multiple sales and upward mobility within your company.

# 13

## Know Your Time and Place

A big part of selling is simply understanding your surroundings, how they affect you, and how you can influence them through your action. In other words, in order to strike the right chord with your target audience, you must understand your time and place. When you are at different events and places, you dress differently, and you may even order a different drink. If you are at a wine and cheese party, you most likely aren't going to order a Miller Lite in shorts and flip-flops. The last time you were at a bar watching a game with your buddies, you didn't order a glass of the house red; my guess is that bar didn't even have a house red wine. In the business world, you have to adapt to your time and place by changing your approach or selling style based on the situation. You need to message appropriately based on the conditions on the ground, and only disrupt the status quo if you intend to, it should never happen by accident.

If I could, let me set the scenario of a jeans and T-shirt customer who doesn't use his Outlook calendar and has never had a business card. Chances are this customer is not looking for an 82-slide PowerPoint presentation, outlining every detail of your product and its benefits. They most likely will not respond well to this approach. I am not saying that they don't want you to have a competent and coherent presentation, you certainly do, because someone who is able to be that casual at work is likely very successful and highly competent, they will expect the same from you. They will still want you to be prepared and respect their business and time. They will likely want to see the key selling points and skip all the flowery language and highly rehearsed selling messages. This customer is likely to want to know how your product or service can help them and will hold you to every single commitment you make from the first sales call to the last.

DOI: 10.4324/9781003218258-13

On the contrary, if you have a coat and tie customer who has sent out a formal RFP to multiple vendors, you don't want to show up with no presentation and just your charm to carry you through the process. That may not even get you in the door, and it certainly won't win you the deal. You should be prepared for every scenario in a highly formal process and have data to back up your answers. They will likely challenge you on every aspect or even worse, quietly, and diligently take notes to try and trip you up during the next step of the presentation. The more formal the process the more important it is to respect and reflect that formality. There will likely be little room for humor or sarcasm. You must be engaging, and charismatic in a formal way, which is no easy task. In my experience, being highly competent and prepared is the best way to separate from the rest of the pack with this type of customer.

You need to understand what the environment is before you walk in the door. Sometimes it is obvious, like wearing formal gear to a wedding or jeans to a ball game, we all know that is the appropriate attire. Just like in the business world, you need to understand the scenario before you prepare for the presentation. If you are not sure (it takes us back to something we have said before), ask! You should have your connection from the inside to give you some insight into what the decision-makers expect from you and the other vendors. Don't be the person who wears jeans and a T-shirt to the private golf club; that won't get you on the course or into the deal. You must prepare yourself properly for every possible scenario, which is the same as having your credentials at the door but in some ways is even more important. This goes far beyond your appearance, it includes how you sit in your chair, what you bring with you into the meeting room and what you present. It is important that everything runs as smoothly as possible. Don't depend on technology; always have your backup, whether it is a flash drive or your colleague on the spot with the backup computer (do both). There is nothing worse than something that was completely preventable sidetracking your progress. In knowing your time and place, you have already been invited to the party, and if you embarrass yourself after you get an invitation, it is even worse than not being invited at all. Let me stress this point: if you get your foot in the door and come unprepared or uneducated on the scene, you will do more damage than if you hadn't been invited to the presentation.

Knowing your time and place is more than just pre-work; it is how you act while the process is ongoing. You need to know when it is time to talk and when it is time to listen, when it is time to be bold and when it is time to swallow your pride and take what the customer is dishing out. If you are in the middle of ongoing issues with your product or service, it may not be the best time to tell the customer about your latest and greatest product. Look at it from their perspective. Let me stress that again, look at it from your customer's perspective. If things are going completely haywire with your customer, offer help, not more work for the client. If your product is causing the distress, you better be there for every sling and arrow, do not hide when things are bad, face the challenge. Don't try and upsell during a crisis with your product. Why would they buy something new from you if they are not happy with their current product or service? Know when it is time to sell and know when it is time to empathize.

You also need to know the history that comes with your customer. It can get really awkward if you talk about how outdated a certain product or service is and then you find out that this customer was an early adopter and absolutely loved the product. Also, you should never speak negatively about other salespeople; you can put this in the "don't bash the competition" category. As bad as you know that particular salesperson is, you have no idea the history between the customer and that individual. If you don't have anything nice to say, don't say anything at all, focus on how good you and your product are and you will end up better off in the long run. This is also true when working with members of your own team. There is always talk of being a member of a team and encouraging a team mentality. I have played organized sports all of my life and always had an issue with a member of my team barking out orders like they were the coach or manager. You need to be sensitive to the team dynamic by making sure you do not bark orders at members of your own team. Be respectful of their responsibilities, and if you feel they need to take an action, be diplomatic when you approach them. They will not respond well if you charge them and tell them they are not doing their job. If the diplomatic approach doesn't work, then you can be more aggressive. That being said, being aggressive does not entitle you to be a jerk. Providing feedback is important, and when providing feedback, it is important to stick to what you have seen, heard, and read from that person. Do not give your opinion or what you "think"; this will lead down a negative path. Stick to the facts that are documented and accessible.

I have always felt you need to respect the chain of command. If you can take care of the situation on your own, do it; if not, bring in the leaders of your team to help. This will cover your backside by making sure they are aware of the issue, and you will avoid the "he said, she said" scenario.

Please make sure you at least make an effort to address the issue prior to bringing it to your manager. If you bring a problem to your boss that you could've easily addressed, you will do more damage to yourself than anything the person who is having the issue will.

One last thing while I am on this topic. I have seen countless numbers of celebrities and athletes say or do something stupid and regret it. A broadcaster said, "You have to remember, all phones are now TV cameras and you have to be guarded with your words and actions." I couldn't agree more, and I have seen and heard of exponentially more businesspeople who have made the exact same mistake. Now your mistake may not end up on TMZ or Outside the Lines, but it may be more damaging to your career than it was to that celebrity. Whether it is fair or not, the fact that you don't dunk like LeBron James or have Brad Pitt's looks makes you much more expendable. Your boss will drop you in a flash if you do or say something truly stupid in front of the wrong person. So, try to follow this rule of thumb; if you say it out loud to yourself and it doesn't sound right, don't repeat it. If you wouldn't be comfortable saying it in front of your boss, don't say it. Now, you can think whatever you like, as long as it doesn't affect your performance or your ability to work with your teammates, but don't verbalize it. I may seem paranoid, but someone you don't want to hear or see you will hear or see you, and I guarantee this person will not keep your words or actions a secret. Remember what we said about having a "big friend"; they will guard your best interests as if they were their own, until you put them in a bad position. Don't abuse a positive relationship with the people you report to by saying or doing something foolish in front of the wrong person. They may still like you, but they will always remember the spot you put them in. It is not unlike the first time your parents witnessed you acting like a fool (likely intoxicated), they still loved you, but they did not like you at that moment in time.

Knowing your time and place is about being aware and mature. I go back to the fact we have two ears, two eyes, and one mouth; use your ears and eyes before your mouth. What you see and hear will tell you when and how to use your mouth. It is also important to be a responsible adult who doesn't need to gossip. I have worked for two of the largest companies in the world and have been amazed that it has felt like a big high school at times. Those who gossip rarely win in the long run and usually flame out once the leadership figures out their game. Know where you are and who is around. Be guarded with your words and actions, it will help you avoid the biggest obstacle many of you have, yourself.

# 14

## *Don't Sulk and Don't Let Others Sulk*

I hate party poopers—the people who come out just to complain about their particular lot in life or to pick apart the party and tell you what you should have done or where you should have gone. I can also say with certainty that no one wants to hang out with Debbie or Daryl downer. I don't socialize to drink away my sorrows; I am there to celebrate even if I am just celebrating being with friends. I have never bought a product from a salesperson who is not excited about what he is selling. I have also never bought from someone who trashes his own product or organization and is using their company as an excuse for their underwhelming performance. When you make a sales presentation to a customer, they have no desire to hear about your bad day and how tough it is to sell in your particular market. Every time you are in front of a client, you need to be the best version of yourself. I am not saying you have to be a cheerleader every day, all day, just don't be negative or as my father always deemed it "realistic." Leave your issues at the door; only bad things will come from bringing your personal problems into the boardroom, and to be perfectly honest, nobody cares about your problems when it comes to their business.

Life is hard and business is even harder. I acknowledge the fact that at certain points in my career I have lost faith in my product or company. I have been frustrated by situations I have been put in and have been even more frustrated when I have put myself in a bad position. Whether it was a manufacturing issue, availability concerns, or bad press, I have never let the situation influence my sale in a negative manner. I will fight to exhaustion to find the positive outcomes of each challenge. You need to look at a challenge as an opportunity to show your customer how good a salesperson you are when times are tough. Quite simply, when things are difficult, it is your time to shine. The challenging times are when we

DOI: 10.4324/9781003218258-14

earn our paycheck; anyone can do this when you have the tailwind, how will you react to a headwind? The dial on the positivity meter needs to be bumped up when times are tough. You can bitch and complain after hours and between sales calls, but when you are on the stage selling, you have to be upbeat and positive. Please note that being positive does not mean ignoring reality, you must recognize when a situation has gone sideways. The positivity you must have is within and it carries you to a point of clarity that is absolutely required when dealing with a bad scenario. If you don't embrace and recognize when things kind of suck, your customer will see you as someone who is full of it and not in touch with their struggles.

I have had year-long delays in my product, I have had bad news about my product on 60 Minutes, and I have had my leadership let me down when I needed them the most. I have found the best way to make it through these tough times is to suck it up and be honest and open with my customer. They need to know what the issue is and what the course of action is to make it right. The second part of that last sentence is critical; you must have a solution or at least a plan that works toward finding the solution. The worst thing that can happen is your customer hears about the bad news from someone other than you, so stay in front or at least at the same pace as the issue. If your customer sees the issue on the nightly news or your competitor informs them of the problem, you have put yourself behind the eight ball. When times are tough, you should be putting in your longest and most intense hours, this is not the time to sleep in or skip the last call of the day.

Some of my favorite moments in my career have been when a customer who is having an issue with my product dismisses any potential competitive threat because I had successfully controlled the message. We had recognized and addressed the issue before any other vendor had even walked through the door. Your customer can deal with bad news; they are adults (well, most of them are). What they can't deal with is feeling that you have been anything less than completely honest with them. If you can get out in front of the problem and control the narrative, you can turn a potentially devastating issue into a growth opportunity. Some people call this crisis management; I call it being a professional.

Meanwhile back at the bar, a pet peeve of mine is when someone is sitting in the corner of the bar licking his wounds when everyone around him is having the time of their life. I want everyone to have their own positive memories from the evening and not be jealous that everyone had a good time except him. When selling, I want everyone involved to have some ownership and look forward to what my product or service has done to make their work life better. You have to be aware of this from the first sales presentation you make with a customer and through the life of that product once it is in the customer's hands. This does not mean you have to dictate someone else's fun. People are allowed to enjoy the party in their own way, it is not up to you to decide how someone enjoys themselves. In the business world, the win is good enough, you don't need the entire organization doing backflips when you walk in, as long as you have won the deal. Enthusiasm out of your customer is a great thing to see, but not required. Remember that your customer's job is to run their business, not buy from you; let sleeping dogs lie, after you have won.

Talk to anyone you can who may be affected by the purchase of your goods, and I mean anyone. It is almost impossible to speak to everyone, but I always try to get as close as possible. If your product is going to make the custodian's job a little easier and you get a chance to share that with them, please do it. You never know who will rise to a point where they can influence your next sale. I deem my sale final when I walk into a customer's facility, and I hear how great my product or service is from everyone who comes in contact with it. I really don't have a problem with people giving me negative feedback on my product, because if they are taking the time to share it with me, they have taken some ownership in the product. It also gives me an opportunity to sell my product to them again and help them troubleshoot the problem they are having. You will also receive a wealth of information from the people who use your product every day, and it is very important that you know what the users are saying about your product on a daily basis. Be present with the people who come in contact with your product every day, only good things came come from these relationships.

Often you will come across an individual who just won't join the party, aka The Party Pooper. He is unhappy with you, your product, or maybe something that has nothing to do with your product. You have to wait for the opportunity to include him in the discussion and when that opportunity presents itself, you must pounce on it. This is a mix of art and science, but invariably your party pooper will start giving you subtle signs that he is ready for you to engage them. Imagine you are at the bar and that one person has been in the corner by himself for two hours; this person hasn't even made eye contact. Then he comes to your side of the bar to order or starts to make eye contact with someone in your group. This is the time to go over and offer him a refill or just strike up a conversation about the game on the big TV screen. You shouldn't be over the top with enthusiasm, but you should acknowledge their effort to participate with at least a small gesture in return.

When I am dealing with a difficult customer, I usually try to have a discussion that has nothing to do with my product. Ideally, I want to talk about something that truly interests him or her. If I can transition to my product later on, that is great; if not I will at least mention my discussion with one of their colleagues who has joined in the "party" from the beginning. Either way, I have broken down the artificial wall that has been set up by the customer, and I have gotten them one step closer to my service or product. As a coach of mine once said, "Once you have them leaning, keep pushing consistently and they will eventually fall." This "leaning" gives you an opportunity to change your approach. If you think you can maintain your prior strategy with this detractor, you are making a mistake. In sales, similar to your social life, you have principles, but you have to be flexible on your approach while maintaining those principles. If you are trying to focus on key benefits of your product and your customer finds something else, they think is a good feature, go with it. Don't be a slave to your goals and message when dealing with a party pooper. Again, it is not up to you to dictate how your product or service improves your customer's work life. If you keep your eyes and ears open this "party pooper" is likely to teach you something about your product, don't interrupt them with your goals and messaging, let them teach you. If you brought your friends to a certain club because they have great music and cheap drinks, but one friend gets excited because they have a "Ms. Pacman" machine next to the bathroom, let your friend have a blast playing the game. It is not what you had exactly hoped for, but at least he is having fun. The key is to try to include everyone you possibly can in your party. There will be a point where you can let them be, either you have accomplished your goal or maybe they are just out of the way now and not taking away from anyone else's positive experience with your product.

Just one warning: I try to include as many people as I can when selling, but I never lose sight of the key people. I will reiterate my agreement with my first sales manager who said, "You should step out of your comfort zone every day. If you get through a day of sales calls and never felt that uncomfortable feeling in your stomach, you didn't do your job." It is easy to find the friendliest face in your account and constantly ask them for feedback. At some point, this will become counterproductive; you have to take care of the people who are truly taking care of you. You want to make sure everyone is having fun at the birthday party, but not at the expense of the guest of honor. Be conscious of the signals the key decision-makers are giving you. Usually, you will have to work to pull information from even your best customers. They are businesspeople first, friendly second, and will always strive to maintain some separation and leverage over you. They will most likely never let you get too close to them, and if they do, it will take years. When you are selling you are constantly walking a tightrope. Once you clear one, there is another one you need to walk out on. I will say it again; selling is a mix of art and science. There are certain rules of selling that have to be followed, but it is up to your interpretation and style on how you produce the finished product. Just make sure you are not too focused on the art or the science, there should be a balance.

# 15

## *Focus on Who Is There, Not Who Isn't*

There have been a number of times in my career when I had set up my ultimate meeting where I had all of my advocates and key customers scheduled so I can close and boom! My key advocate or even worse the key decision-maker pulled a no-show at the meeting. This is distressing and it takes everything in your power not to show your disappointment. This reminds me of one particular time when I had a St. Patrick's Day party with some old friends coming in town for it. I had one friend whom I was particularly excited to see and his commitment to be a part of the day had my excitement levels through the roof! This was a guy we had all lost touch with since college, so this was the big reunion. Literally about ten minutes into the party, I got a text message: "Sorry man, not going to make it." I was really disappointed, mostly because I thought this was a great chance to get the crew back together again. Now, I had to take a look around and notice I had some of my best friends in the world around me, and we were going to drink multiple green cocktails. This was not the time to focus on who wasn't there, but rather to enjoy the people who were there for the party. In the business world, you will rarely, if ever, get all the people you need and want in the same room, you must not let someone who is not attending the meeting negatively influence your performance.

It is a little easier to not worry about those who are absent from a party than it is an important business meeting, but you have to be able to move past this tough situation. Usually, if someone skips your sales presentation, either he is not interested in the product or he feels he is above this part of the process. Either way, getting the people who are there for the presentation excited for your product is the best way for you to pique the interest of your no-show. You need to sell hard to the people at the meeting. You can be 99.9% sure that one, if not all, of the people at that

DOI: 10.4324/9781003218258-15

meeting has been saddled with reporting back to the key decision-maker. If you go through the motions with the "other guys," the news of your bad attitude will spread back to those holding the checkbook. Conversely, if you sell the people in that room with passion and enthusiasm, the word will spread back just as quickly. The lower-level players will bring a sense of urgency back to their bosses and will most likely lead to a one-on-one selling situation with the key decision-maker. A Broadway performer does not tailor their performance to the audience, they go on stage every night and give it their all every night. You must have the same mentality for your sales calls. You will have plenty of time to decompress between calls and meetings, but when you're in the arena, you must be completely committed to giving your best effort, regardless of the audience.

Another thing to keep in mind is that just because you think the "key" player isn't there, doesn't mean you are correct. You may be under the impression that the CEO makes the final decision on purchases, when in actuality the department head makes the final call. If you work off this false assumption and come in with a B minus performance, you will be dead in the water. I have done this a number of times in my social life; I pull a group of people together and try to include a person I think is well-liked by the group. When the person can't make it, I find out during the evening that my thoughts were wrong, and if that person had shown up, it would have taken away from the others. We must sell to anyone who may touch your product or service, right? I don't care who is in the room, what level of importance you think they have; you sell them and sell them hard. Do you think when Tiger or MJ are out there playing for "fun" they take it easy on their opponents? I know for a fact that Tiger will give a scratch golfer between 12 and 15 strokes and dare them to take it. There is no "coast mode" in sales; I get pumped when I talk to my family about my products. Why would I ever limp into a sales presentation when I have bills to pay? I wouldn't, and you shouldn't either.

If you pull your punches in a meeting every person in the room will remember you in a negative way. Now, you may still be able to pull through the deal after you get some time with this particular key decision-maker, and that is obviously great. But what happens when one of those people in that room is promoted within that organization or the decision-maker moves on? I promise you that one day, a new person will be holding the purse strings, and you will pay dearly for not treating him or her with respect in the past. Because when you don't sell at the highest level when in front of a group of people, you disrespect them, and they will always remember you treated them that way. If you step on the heads of people to reach your goals and not acknowledge how much they helped you, you are bound to regret it.

So don't worry about who isn't in the room. You owe every person there your utmost focus and effort. Pardon my language, but if you half-ass it, that is exactly where you will get kicked.

# 16

## *Have a Full Wallet*

Nothing is more embarrassing than promising the people in your party the best night ever and when the evening comes, you under-deliver. You also can't run up a $10,000 tab and expect to cover the expenses on your credit card that has a $5,000 limit. In the business world, you need to make sure you set reasonable expectations whether you are dealing with your customers, colleagues, or bosses. If you tell them you are going to do something by a certain date or at a certain level and do not deliver on the promise, it tells them you are not of value or, even worse, you purposely deceived them. One of the worst things you can do is leave your customer with the thought that you have pulled the bait-and-switch on them. In the same vein, if you inflate the value of a deal or accelerate the timeline of a deal and come up short, you will lose the faith of the person who needs to have unwavering confidence in you. You can't buy rounds of Belvedere for everyone in your party and expect to pay Bud Light prices. If you are willing to stick your neck out and make big promises, it is up to you to come through. The flip side of this is when you promise big and deliver, you accelerate your position in any organization you are a part of.

One of the mistakes I made earlier in my career was to assume that just because my customer asked a question about my product that they actually wanted that feature. It was a test, and I learned the hard way that they were trying to trip me up or find out how well I knew my own product. I made the mistake of promising something my product couldn't do and then had to come back to that customer with my tail between my legs, conceding price and an upgrade to appease the customer. Not good. Truth is a hard and fast rule; you must always remain truthful while setting expectations. If your product can't perform what the customer is requesting or your service can't give the customer what they want, tell

DOI: 10.4324/9781003218258-16

them upfront. It will allow you to move the discussion where you want it to go and tell them why, even though your product comes up short in one area, another benefit makes up for it and then some. If you lie to your customer, they buy your product and realize you were not honest, you will lose that customer for a very long time. Your career cannot be a series of short-term gains with negative long-term effects; a burn-the-fields mentality to business will always lead you down a bad path. It is likely that the word will spread to other customers, and you will feel the effects of this for an extended period of time. Even if you had lost the deal but told the truth, you would have lived to fight another day. Remember that losses will happen, if you are not truthful you will lose the opportunity to position yourself for the next deal.

There are times when you make commitments based on what your company tells you they can do and once you win, your organization lets you down on what they said you can deliver. This is a difficult situation to handle and unfortunately likely to happen at one point in your career. You will still be responsible in the eyes of the customer, but at least you can explain the circumstances. First, tell your customer the very moment you realize you can't deliver on your commitments. Your customers are adults; they want to hear good news fast and bad news immediately. Don't play games, just be upfront and take the heat. Second, don't blame the organization or trash your company. This would put doubt in the customer's head. Be prompt and honest when you fall short of your commitments, and you will be better off in the long run. The key is not having the solution in this scenario; the key is having an achievable plan to find the solution.

If you are visiting Los Angeles or New York, you will see people run out of money because they paid too much to get in the door. Every city has ultra-exclusive establishments that either require significant funds to enter or require $1,000 bottle service. If the bar has a $50 cover and you have $55 in your pocket, you will get in the door, but that is about it. Sometimes the price of admission is just too high, and you have to walk away. If this is a customer looking for 10,000 units in 60 days, and your company can only deliver 100 a month, it may not be worth going after that whale of a deal. Your best-case scenario is to find your niche with the customer and supply 100 a month over the course of a year while your organization ramps up. You can have the greatest product in the world, but if you can't do the simple things like meet the minimum requirements on the order, you will overpay at the door, leaving nothing left to play with once you are inside. There is nothing wrong with being the secondary supplier if your company can't handle the large volume deals. This will keep your foot in the door and allow your organization to grow and meet what large deals demand.

More often than not, price is something you give away to get in the door of a new customer. When lowering the price, you usually are dealing with a competitive stronghold, or you have an inferior product. The problem is you may get your foot in the door with this bottom basement price, but you lack the quality or allegiance to your product to get you to the finish line, or at least to get you across the finish line on the next deal. You often win once on price; the next time price alone won't be enough. It is always better to develop an advocate over time than going in and trying to buy the business. I have often taken the opposite approach in a competitive account. I will work hard to develop an advocate in the account and then come in with a price that is much higher than what I can offer and much higher than my competition. It doesn't always work all of the time, but in my view, when you are in a competitive account, what do you have to lose? If you have sold properly, you can position your product as a high-value, premium product and then drop your price to a reasonable level during the negotiation process. Do not take wild price swings in the dark in an attempt to win business. If you think your boss was tough when you ask to approve the price, wait until you lose at aggressive prices. If you make a price swing, your confidence level must be very high to deploy the strategy and you better make sure the client knows this is "special, one-time introductory pricing"; I have even gone as far to show them the price on the next unit, just to level set the client.

The last part of having a full wallet is making sure you have a knowledge base that is needed to sell once you are in the door. You need to be a product expert or, at the very least, a features and benefits expert in order to have credibility with any client. A baseline level of knowledge is needed to get past the "doorman," but this has to be stepped up a notch when you are selling to the "bartenders" or decision-makers. If you are selling to the decision-makers, you not only need to know your product, but also need to know the economic and strategic selling strategies for the leadership within that account. A CEO may care how your product works and how it is better than the competition, but he is more concerned about how it puts them in an advantageous position versus their competition or positions them for the future. I do not expect you to become a technical expert like your engineers, but you should have enough working knowledge for your customers to wonder if you are an engineer. You wouldn't buy a car from someone who couldn't tell you the horsepower and gas mileage of the vehicle, would you? Well, neither will your customer if they don't have confidence that you know your product.

Having a full wallet includes more than just price: it is knowledge and understanding capabilities. There is no point tapping yourself out to just get in the room. Make sure if you are in the room, you have enough in your pocket to reach your goals and to satisfy your customer's needs. Once you have gotten in the room keep in mind how large your "toolbox" is and make sure you don't get too far outside of your domain knowledge. You also need to be a strong enough resource for the customer that they feel they can take advanced questions to you and get an answer. If you don't know, be honest and tell the customer, "I am not sure, but I will ask my team and get back to you as soon as possible." You don't need all the answers, but you better have most of them.

# 17

## Buy a Round

In the business world and in your personal life, you should buy drinks for others early and often. Buying a round comes in a number of different forms and fashions. The best way I can think of buying a round is to share your knowledge and experience with someone within your network or organization. There will be times when you want to share your experience with someone and buy them a drink, and they will have no interest in accepting it. This person may not be worth the time or effort, or you just need to push a little harder to get through to them or just wait. There will be certain individuals who will resist at first, but it will be worth your time to wait until they come back and ask for your advice. Either way, buying a drink can be the most fulfilling thing you can do for your mentee and yourself. I have had mentors give me "pearls" about themselves, but even more impactful have told me stories about people who were an influence on them. I had one manager tell me he had a colleague who would find "the one thing" that the customer really wanted and continue to focus on that until the deal was done. One of these pearls was the inspiration for this book. I have accepted the drinks that people have bought for me in my career and used their advice every day. Also, please don't forget to tip and tip well. The best tip I know of is sincere gratitude. There are some great ways to "tip" and say thank you that we will touch on later.

You can also buy drinks in other ways. One other great way is to share your experience about specific customers and pointers on how they can be handled effectively by others. Some who were difficult and how I managed to win their business. Others who were loyal to me and my product became the key to my sales success. I like to use phrases like "In my experience," "Keep your eye out for," or "Take this with a grain of salt" when speaking about customers in order to not completely cloud the

DOI: 10.4324/9781003218258-17

judgment of the person I am trying to help. Just because that particular customer didn't buy from me, doesn't mean they won't buy from you as a new salesperson. Quite often a new colleague's approach will be more effective than anything done by the jaded businesspeople we are at times. When you are helping someone out with customers, do not be emotional. Give the facts and figures, key contacts, key decision-makers, and what the selling environment is. You don't need to tell him about how unreasonable a certain character in the account is, you must help them, not tell them to avoid knocking on that door.

One of the most important drinks you can buy is knowledge about your own organization and how to maneuver through it. I call this learning how to be a house cat. House cats become comfortable with their indoor surroundings, never stray far from the people who feed them, and find a way to ingratiate themselves into the fabric of a family and their home. In most companies, you need to be a house cat from time to time. No matter how big or small the company is, there are always quirks and cliques that can be very difficult to deal with. Buy a new person a drink and tell him whom to contact when you need to get a legal question answered. Whom to call with an issue with your expense report or a question about pricing strategy. Tell him who to watch out for and who can be a resource with product questions. Give the information that you had to learn the hard way. Don't be the person who says, "I had to learn the hard way, he can too." Be a resource for the people around you and make sure you are available to those seeking out your help.

On the other side of the coin, the most successful people I know are more like outdoor cats. An outdoor cat doesn't depend on others for food, shelter, or warmth. They are comfortable being alone on an island. Many of the successful people I have worked with have no issue going it alone or with a small group of highly trusted people. You can be a house cat and move your way up to a comfortable management role in a company, but usually it's the outdoor cats that tend to be more entrepreneurial and the true leaders in the organization. If you are an "outdoor cat" and giving advice, please be sure to tell your mentee that being this type of business professional can often be the hardest path to take. There will be times you question your decisions and wonder if you were too confident in your own abilities. The downside is also much worse in this life, but the upside is virtually unlimited. There is no right answer, and you need to understand if you are a person who craves stability or change. If you want stability above all else, you may be a house cat. That being said, you need to have elements of both house and outdoor cat to be successful in business and life. Balance is the key.

This brings me to my last point under this topic. I have always been amazed that the most successful people who I have worked with or had the privilege to speak with have been the most likely to lend advice to those who seek it out. When you are buying a drink for someone, it is because they need it. You are not buying a drink for a woman with three drinks in front of her; you are buying drinks for people who are thirsty. In the business world, they are thirsty for knowledge, fill their glass, and fill it with high-end stuff. There is nothing more transparent than halfhearted advice, it will not positively impact the person who is receiving the advice. Never be too big to be a resource to someone who needs it. You also don't want to push your advice or experiences on everyone you work with, you need to take different approaches to how you give advice. It is similar to mirroring your client. If the colleague seeking your guidance does so with enthusiasm, they will likely want more anecdotes and more details. If they are more reserved the approach or haven't approached you at all, it would be better to give them small points of guidance at opportune, non-threatening times. The advice will be much better received when the time is right. I do not know anyone who responds well to advice that sounds like "I told you so." Read the person seeking advice and give them your full attention, as your mentors did for you.

# 18

## Never, Ever Turn Down a Free Drink

Turning down a free drink is just rude, pure and simple. If someone offers you a drink, never, ever turn it down, even if you have no intention of drinking the free cocktail. You don't have to take it down with two gulps, but if someone is kind enough to spend their money on you, let them. Think of it as a gift, you wouldn't hand a Christmas present back to someone who took the time to purchase and wrap it for you; a free drink is a gift you should accept. In the business world, you will be offered "free drinks" early and often; you should never turn these down either. There will be times when you won't want advice or training; force yourself to take it or at least listen to it. There will also be no shortage of opportunities to observe and learn from your colleague's styles and strategies; these are bonus drinks as far as I am concerned. You can learn just as much from your colleagues' successes and mistakes as you can from your own. All of these opportunities to drink for free should be capitalized on and put into your bank of knowledge for later use.

We spoke earlier about "the locals"; they are the ones most likely to buy you a free round. They will do this in a number of ways. Usually, it is some way to maneuver through the internal politics of your job or how to handle a difficult customer. This advice is often unsolicited and usually not very useful at that moment in time. There is a good chance that you will never use that advice, but if the time comes, you will be very happy that you stuck around and gave that person your attention. You let them "buy you a drink" and now it has paid dividends that result in reduced headaches for you, all without having to go through a tough lesson on your own. Many of the stories I have shared in this book have been a result of unsolicited advice that I put in the parking lot until it was time to take it out for a ride. It is like accepting a free drink that you have no intention

DOI: 10.4324/9781003218258-18

of finishing. You put a nipple on it and nurse it all night, maybe you need to drive home or perhaps you tied one on the night before and just can't stomach another drink. The key is that you were polite and accepted it. Not only have you picked up some knowledge, but you have also gained some admiration from the person buying the drink. They are obviously proud of what they are sharing, or they would have kept it to themselves. By you being engaged with this individual you have increased their self-worth by valuing their information, and you have enriched yourself with new information, so everyone wins! Now, if you accept this drink half-heartedly, you will be in danger of irking that person and turning them against you. At the very least, you owe your undivided attention to the person you are getting advice from, so make good eye contact and ask questions. Even if you feel that you could get better sales advice from your 10-year-old nephew, an ounce of attention will be worth its weight in gold to the advice-giver and, again, it is just the polite thing to do.

Now, there will be times when you are dying for a certain individual to buy drinks. Perhaps they have the hookup to the VIP or in the business world they have been and still are a top performer and you are bone-dry when it comes to new strategy and technique. I find when these people "buy drinks," it is top-shelf knowledge, and it is worth its weight in platinum. You can't be a mooch, but you have to take the information that these individuals share and put it into action. Sometimes this is tough; you are most likely highly competitive with this individual and you have tried to discount them a little in your own head to help your own ego. I have said it before, check your emotions at the door. If this person is whooping your ass every quarter, you need to listen to them, or at the very least observe their actions closely. Sometimes the "bought drink" is simply a true professional in action. Don't be jealous or undermining, embrace how good your fellow businessperson is, and go to school on how they do their job, interact with their manager, and handle difficult client issues.

Which brings me to my next piece of advice: steal at will. If you see something that you like and is working for one of your colleagues, do not be too proud to do the exact same thing. I only jumped behind one bar in my life to "liberate" a bottle. Fortunately for me, it worked out fine, meaning I got away with it without getting my head bashed in by a bouncer. I have on more than one occasion buddied up to the guy with the wide-open tab on the Platinum card and extracted a few drinks for me and some friends. If I see or hear of someone being successful using a selling technique or strategy, you better believe I steal that thing and use it right away. My bank account does not have an ego, and as a result, I have quickly realized that there is much to be gained from learning from those around you. This could be something small, a witty opening line or a penetrating question that paints the customer into the corner. I don't care how small and insignificant; I will steal it. Often, I will steal an idea that an individual cannot fully develop but once I hear it, I know exactly which way to go to knock it out of the park. Call me immature, but I like being better at things than the people I work around, and I like the idea that I may at times intimidate those around me whether they are on my team or not. The ability to create, develop, and execute a sales strategy is one of the hardest things we do as businesspeople. There are always the one-hit wonders and people who have great ideas, but just can't put them into effect. There are salespeople who are extremely organized and eloquent when messaging but can't develop their own plans. The top performers can do it all; they have all facets of sales under control and wear out their competition because they are a complete package. The top performers are most likely not rock stars in every required skill set, but they have no big holes in their skill set. Businesspeople who always deliver are also more likely to lean on what they do best. One of my biggest mentors always told me, "There is a reason that home run hitters don't practice bunting." Make sure you take full advantage of your strongest qualities; top performers do, and that is why they have been consistent high performers and why you should listen to them when they are "buying drinks."

Training and sales meetings are two things that I used to enjoy and now really don't enjoy. I now get pissed off every time I have to fly or drive to these meetings. I say this as I am on a plane for training. Have you ever seen what happens to a group of outside salespeople when they are stuck in a hotel conference room or classroom for a week or, God forbid, two weeks? It turns into a 9th-grade study hall. The texting, whispering secrets, and stupid giggling just drive me nuts. It is a group of people that is completely out of their element and that is why you see so many crazy things happening at these meetings. You name it, I have seen it. The random hook-ups, the adulterous affairs, the drunken belligerence. My next book may be a collection of stories about what I have witnessed and been a part of in different sales training and meetings in my career. As much as I have come to dislike these meetings, you have to take them as free drinks as well. Sales training really is the building blocks of your style that will develop over time. You need to know the principles. It is kind of like writing (something I know nothing about, as you may have guessed); there are basic rules that have to be followed, but they should not dictate your style. Product training can be painful as well, but if you are like me, it is the only time you will truly devote to growing your knowledge base. I usually pick things up as I go, but when you are forced into a week-long training and you really dig into it, you truly strengthen yourself as a salesperson. It is also a chance for you to get some exposure to people who are usually pretty connected within your organization. Most sales training operations are located at headquarters and the trainers usually have a network that is extensive. If you want to move up in your organization, you need to be a superstar when you are at training. The better you perform in these setting, the better positioned you will be for promotions and career advancing project, so take advantage of the time spent at these gatherings.

Sales meetings are also on my sh—list. The worthless assignments, the territory planning, and the overall rah-rah attitude make my skin crawl at times. I am guilty of this myself; my first sales meeting as a manager was peppered with inspirational quotes, lofty goals, and motivational exercises. I have to laugh when I look back. Jim Valvano, the famous N.C. State basketball coach, had a story about stealing a speech from Vince Lombardi, where Vince said and I paraphrase, "there are only three things that matter this year, your God, your Family, and The Green Bay Packers." Valvano had intended to change the Green Bay Packers to N.C. State Wolfpack. In the locker room before the first game Valvano pulled his team together and said, "Gentlemen, there are three things that matter this year, your God, your Family, and The Green Bay Packers"! Jim went on to have a tremendous career because he had passion, but he took it too far his first time out, and so did I. With all that being said, sales meetings are a great place to steal ideas. You will hear every single story about how your teammates had the best plan, the best presentation, and the best result. Most of it is complete crap, but you likely pull away at least a few ideas to take back out into the field with you. If I can toot my own horn here, I am a master of sales meetings, mainly because I stay engaged. As much as I hate them, I know that it is one of those necessary evils and if you perform well during them, you can do great things for your career. I can honestly say that all my managers ended up becoming my friends. I am extremely low maintenance and reliable and I perform very well when the lights are shining bright. When you are at a sales meeting, your bosses are constantly comparing you among yourselves, and if they say they aren't, they are lying. They want to see who knows their business, who knows the product, and who knows how to play the game without looking like they are playing the game. Sales meetings are the quickest and most effective ways to impress your boss and their bosses. If you come prepared, stay engaged, and don't do anything stupid, you will reap huge benefits. You can also shoot yourself in the foot at these meetings. If you are overly negative, critical, or just an overall pain in the ass, your sales number will not protect you. If your boss doesn't like you, he will be dismissive when your numbers are good and all over you when your numbers are even mediocre. If you are a brown nose, you will lose the respect of your teammates and eventually the respect of the person who you are giving the nose job to. My best advice for how to make it through sales meetings is to be a positive version of yourself. I give the same advice to people going into interviews: just be the most positive version of yourself you can be, and you will be just fine. And please don't be the drunk at the meeting. I try to be the middle drunk at the sales meeting, I don't want to be the guy stumbling from table to table, but I also don't want to be the guy in bed at 8:30. There is no hard and fast number of drinks that I can recommend, but a word of advice is to follow your boss's or best performers drinking pace. I have stumbled home from the bar with my colleagues, but I have always been with my boss. I have even had to go back to a bar the next morning to search for my manager's lost business AMEX on one occasion. That particular manager is still a friend of mine and that whole night was stinking hilarious, so I give us both a pass on that one.

You have to take those free drinks when they come your way. You can't be prideful or dismissive of someone who is willing to share what they have learned with you. All of this information is important, even if you can't use it at the time, there is value there. You will get a feel of the person who is buying the drinks, you will increase your knowledge base, and you will gain some respect all at the same time. It is a win-win and even if you don't have any intention of drinking the free drink, you always have it just in case. If there is one rule of them when it comes to all the scenarios where you may get "free drinks," it is to be engaged and give people the attention they are due, they are trying to help you, let them.

# 19

## Be on the Prowl

I was once a single guy; many of you are single or at least have a vague recollection of what was like to be single. Even more of you have a distorted view of what your life was like when you were single. I am sure that no matter how prim and proper you were or at least thought you were, you occasionally went out with the intention of meeting someone who you could date or even just spend an evening with, and, to be clear, I am not judging this type of activity. It is a part of single life and part of the process of being single and foolish. Hopefully, you didn't do anything that caused you any permanent damage; my guess is that you probably look back on those days or maybe even last night and shake your head or maybe just laugh a bit. For those of you like me who have found the love of your life and have settled down, you understand that single life, although fun, doesn't give you the kind of fulfillment a relationship does. On the other hand, there are some things that the single life gives you that are unique to that lifestyle and don't come in a long-term relationship. The pursuit of your career—mind you I said career, not job—is very similar to the single life. You may have to venture down a number of different paths before you find "the one." The key is recognizing which path is long-term and sustainable and which are more fleeting. Even a short-term job is a great place to learn and get you ready to settle down in a career sense.

For those of you who aren't married, let me fill you in on a few things. If you are in a good marriage, it will complete your life, it will give you everything you give to it and so much more. That being said, it is not always easy. There will be times of conflict and a number of challenges to overcome, but the positives far outweigh the negatives. On the other hand, if you are in a bad relationship, it will tear you apart from the inside. It will bleed into every other facet of your life and make what you used to

DOI: 10.4324/9781003218258-19

be great, terrible. That is why it is critically important to make sure you pick the right person to share the rest of your life with. It is much easier to change your career than it is to change your spouse, and as a matter of policy, it is better to not change either too many times.

There are many parallels between your marriage and your career. Picking the right career will make everything else in your life better, while picking the wrong career will slowly make what was once good, bad. There is a big difference between a girlfriend or boyfriend (job) and a wife or husband (career). Any idiot can get a girlfriend or job; it is usually something that helps you pass the time while giving you some sort of empty benefit like a paycheck or sex. A career or life partner will fulfill you on a much deeper level; it is more than just money or sex. It helps you develop as a person; it gives you perspective and clears your judgment. A job is just that, a task, a career is your lot in life, something that inspires passion and doesn't even feel like work most of the time. In short, a career is your professional identity, much like your marriage is your personal identity. It is important that you go into your career with your eyes wide open to what you are committing to and for how long. Your day-to-day activity is something you must enjoy or there is no way to make it a career.

I don't want anyone out there who hasn't yet found their career to freak out because of the last paragraph. If you haven't found the work that inspires your passion yet, there is no shortage of time or opportunity to find it. Some people find their career when they are children. Many people know they want to be a doctor or lawyer when they are 13 years old and work their entire lives to realize that goal. Other people barely know how to tie their shoes when they are that age and will figure out their career path much later. You can have a job for 30 years and not have a career; I have seen a number of people who don't start their career until they have been in the workforce for multiple decades. Most people have had to make mistakes and try out a bunch of different jobs before they find their career. Neither path is better or correct, they are just different. For example, my best friend knew that he wanted to marry a certain girl, that he wanted to go to the Naval Academy and become a pilot, when we were freshmen in high school. Nine years later, he was a Naval Academy graduate, married to that woman, and in flight school. I, on the other hand, tried to date every single type of girl there was on the planet, stumbled into a decent school, played collegiate, then professional golf, and took me an even longer time to finally meet a woman who would stick with me for more than six months.

My friend and I both have the career we want, the family we want, and are happy; my friend just knew what he wanted and found it before I did. We had very different experiences; we learned from each other's mistakes and successes and are better people and husbands for it today. Everyone's career path is different; some people make it harder on themselves than necessary by picking the wrong path and change direction mid-stream and, unfortunately, some people never find their path and wander through their life. I believe the biggest factor for those who don't find their career is fear. They are afraid to commit to their lot in life, or even worse they don't recognize what they are good at and pursue it. Another common mistake is going into a field because they feel pressure to do it from an outside agency like their parents or friends from school. Either way, if you choose a career or a partner because you think it is "what you are supposed to do," I will lay big money on failure for that individual, or at the very least they will lack joy when it comes to their career. You need to know who you are as a person and choose your career path based on that understanding. If you are the kind of person who *has* to try everything once, you will probably hop from job to job for a while until you find your career path. If you crave stability, you will most likely be much happier if you find what your passion is before you start taking random jobs which is likely to make you miserable. Just remember, if you choose the wrong career path it is not the end of the world. If you see yourself going down the wrong path, abandon ship and reevaluate. Maybe you need to go back to school. I have to say, I have seen a number of people stop selling and go to law school and get their master's in education or some other field of interest. More often than not, they come away much happier people. What I suggest though, is that you don't change career paths for money. Don't get me wrong, money is important, but if you can feed yourself, clothe yourself, and put a roof over your head, that is all the money you need if you are passionate about what you do. Regardless of your chosen career, you have to accept, embrace, and enjoy the everyday activity at work.

I am sure you're saying, "Alright genius, how do I pick a career?" First of all, I don't have all or even most of the answers, but just like in love, your career often finds you. You just have to be willing to accept it. I know that sounds very philosophical, i.e., BS, but in my experience that is the case. You have to be willing to accept the opportunity of your career and then work relentlessly to attain it. Just know that there will be major obstacles in your way and that is a good thing. Yes, a good thing, if it was easy, you would be doing it already. You also have to be willing to accept the fact that no career is perfect. If you are waiting for the $500k-a-year job with great hours, no boss, and no investment, good luck. I suspect you will be waiting for a long time to find a career that meets that standard. To use the title of this chapter, always be on the prowl. Spend time with people who love their job, not because you will be happy doing the same thing, but because you will gain insight into why what they are doing makes them happy. I will bet another large sum of money that they are happy because they have passion and believe in what they are doing, not because they make big bucks. When you are "on the prowl" in the business world, you are looking for opportunities to fulfill yourself. It is likely a balance of money, where your talents lie, and your ability to impact a given situation. Have you ever heard a person talk about their significant other and say, "We were friends for a long time and then one day it just hit me, this is the person I am supposed to be with"? I have found that many times, your career path is right in front of you, but you have to have your eyes and ears open to find it.

I mentioned fear earlier; most people are afraid of "settling down" because they see it as giving up in some way. Sometimes your career is your job; you just don't know it yet. In many ways, your professional life will replace your single life once you are married. You no longer go out to bars looking for a companion for the evening; you have all you want and more at home. So, instead of searching for a potential significant other, you should now speak to strangers who you think are successful to see if you can "hook up" with them and further your career. As I said before, you have to be self-aware in order to make good decisions. When it comes to a career change, you have to weigh what you want versus what you already have in your current role. It is like having a long-term significant other and being tempted by someone new. If you are smart, you will weigh each option and make a decision that isn't based on some short-term emotion. It is similar when you have a job that you like but aren't sure that you want it for your career. You can and should be on the prowl for other opportunities, but you have to evaluate the positives and negatives of both what you have and make a non-emotional decision on the career path you may want to pursue. It is very possible that your current job provides the best possible career path for you. Whichever way you decide to go, you must pursue that career path fiercely and never look back. Just make sure you don't burn turn many bridges if you decide to leave your current role, it is possible that you may want to go back or have the opportunity to do business with your current colleagues in your new role. So please leave as many doors open as possible, even if you leave your job.

One last thing about "settling down": this term is the biggest crock that I can think of when it comes to your career. Just because you have decided that this is your chosen path, does not mean you have settled. You have merely picked the area in which you will devote all of your focus and passion. You have now entered the fun part of your professional life; you have the opportunity to soar to your greatest heights because you are no longer distracted by what else is out there. However, you must still be on the prowl, once you have chosen your career path. Not searching for growth opportunities once you have chosen your career path would be like getting married and no longer working to help that relationship blossom. If you take this attitude when you pick a career or a mate you will be in deep trouble, saddling yourself with a mediocre existence. You haven't settled, you have focused and now you need to be on the prowl for growth opportunities on your chosen career path. You can also continue to prowl for greater opportunities within that career path, but in a different organization or by branching out on your own. When someone tells me that they have had settled into a position, I know that person is done growing. Don't be the person who was once hungry and pursued career advancement at every turn but has now "settled" and is more likely to say, "I don't care" when presented with challenges and opportunities. Even when you have picked your career, you should continue to seek ways to be as successful as you can be in that particular lot in life. The learning and growth curve is never-ending based on my work with very successful people. These people never assume they know it all or have accomplished everything they are capable of. The most successful people I know continue to stay on the prowl and go out of their way to find new solutions and opportunities. Here is a little homework for you. Think of the three most successful people you can think of and dig into where they invest their time and money. Whether they are a titan of industry or a professional athlete, I guarantee you that they have taken on business and personal ventures outside of their core talents. Take this as a definite cue that in order to be successful, you must seek out new challenges, even after you have picked your career path.

# 20

## Confidence Is King, Arrogance Is the Jester

Just so we are all perfectly clear, you will not find me on the cover of *GQ* any time soon. I am by no means a model, nor do I have an incredible physique. I am just a regular dude and could be any one of a thousand faces that you will see in the bar. If you were of a certain persuasion, you most likely wouldn't even look twice at me when I walk by. I wasn't a model in college either; most people put on "the freshman fifteen," well, I put on a freshman sixty, topping out at roughly 250 pounds. I eventually dropped that weight, and of course now that I am getting older, I have started losing my hair. I am kind of making myself sound like the elephant man, but the point is I will not be doubling for Brad Pitt any time soon. With all of these shortcomings, I have married a beautiful woman, against all odds! Even when I was in the heavyweight division in college, I somehow managed to date attractive women. Why am I telling you this? Because I know that the only reason I was able to meet and gain the interest of women when I was single and somehow manage to talk to my wife into walking down the aisle is that I have always been confident and secure in who I am. Every great salesperson I know is married to someone far more attractive, or at the very least as attractive as they are. My friends and I call it "outkicking your coverage." On the other hand, I have seen a large number of very attractive but extremely arrogant people strike out constantly with members of the opposite sex. The bottom line is that people are attracted to confidence and repulsed by arrogance. When someone behaves in an arrogant manner, it has the opposite effect of when someone is confident. There is no charisma in arrogance; at most, you may have people follow you out of fear and that is short term at best, there is no loyalty.

DOI: 10.4324/9781003218258-20

The tough part about arrogance versus confidence is that there is a very fine line between the two and many people will confuse one with the other. Sometimes your customer will call you arrogant when you do small things like saying "when" instead of "if." If I were to define confidence in my terms, I would say that confidence is having the strength to stick to your convictions. It is being willing to tell your customers that they need to change what they are doing, i.e., what they are doing is wrong without offending them. Confidence is a fragile thing, it is kind of like trust, hard to obtain and easy to lose. The truly great salespeople do lose their confidence from time to time, but they never allow their customer to see it. They stay confident that their product is the best fit for the customer, and they power through times of self-doubt through hard work.

I have been through more ups and downs with my products that I can count. While I have acknowledged the issues with my customers, I always maintained the confidence that my product and organization would be better and stronger when the problem has resolved. That being said, I have lost accounts because I could not overcome my or my product's issues. When I have lost accounts, I have continued to go into the fire of a competitive account and sell them again on the benefits of my product or service. You also have to have the courage to put your neck out on the line for your product. You have to be willing to say, "Give my product one chance, if it doesn't do what I say it does you will never see me again." Customers are constantly trying to rattle their salespeople. Many of them get their rocks off by using the power to fluster and discourage you. I always picture the smart kid in high school who had a chip on his shoulder about not making the basketball team. Now, that person runs the department that you are selling in, and they are going to get their revenge. You absolutely cannot lose your cool or back off any of the statements that you have made about your product or service. If you do, you will definitely wave goodbye to that sale. Similar to sports, the more you practice selling, the more confident you are going to end up. Whether it is military or elite level sports, you will hear them say how hard they practice. They do this to make sure when the pressure is on, they do not see the drop in performance that their competition experiences. You must first practice to be confident and win.

Arrogance is like bad breath; it is rare that someone recognizes they have it and therefore never do anything to correct it. The only time you recognize the fact that you have bad breath is if someone tells you. If you are lucky, it is someone who cares about you and performs an intervention of sorts. More likely, it will be someone who has no desire to talk to you and comes up with, "Do you know how bad your breath smells?" Ouch, that hurts, and if you are even a little self-aware, it will stick with you for a long time. People around you will tell you if you are arrogant, by how they react to you. Do they tend to undermine or minimize your work? Does it always feel like people are talking about you? If you don't see and hear loyalty from your colleagues, you may have the stench of arrogance.

I have seen this quite often; a salesperson has a good or even superior product but still loses deals to another vendor. There are only two reasons for this: your price is too high, and if I'm being honest, that can't be the case if you have sold properly and shown the true value of your product. If your customer truly wants your product, they will beg, borrow, and steal to buy it from you. More likely, the customer asked for follow-up and didn't get it or you demonstrated in some other way that your time was too precious to waste on them. Your arrogance pushed the customer into another vendor's arms. Arrogance comes in many forms and, more often than not, is not done intentionally. I just mentioned follow-up; if your customer asks you to do something and you agree to do it, you are officially on the hook. If you forget about the request or choose not to follow up, your customer will see you as arrogant or even worse, incompetent. I have found that a lack of follow-up is the easiest way to be given the label of arrogant salesperson. When you don't follow up, you are neglecting to perform a basic function of a salesperson, listening!

A less common and more deadly type of arrogance is when a salesperson thinks he or she is being confident by telling the customer what they should or are going to do. Remember, you are essentially telling the customer that what they are doing is wrong and your solution is better. Now, we all would love to say, "Hey idiot, stop spending too much money for an inferior product, now give me my PO so I can go take care of someone that isn't so dumb." Just some friendly advice, I would try to temper your remarks when you are selling to a difficult customer. Stick to the facts, talk about your product's features, and don't bash their current vendor, which by the way was your customer's decision. You must remember that someone in that account or in that meeting room made the decision to go with their current vendor. You have to keep that in mind when selling against your competition if you don't you will essentially call someone a moron and not realize it. Avoid saying things like, "When you buy the product or when we install the system or after you place your first order." You are trying to project confidence, but what you are really doing is telling the customer that they are not capable of making a decision on their own. How would you like it if the next time you go to buy a car, the salesperson says, "When you buy the red car" after you have made it clear that you are there to buy a black car? Arrogance is rarely blatant. Arrogance is usually subtle; it has a cumulative effect and if it doesn't cost you on this deal, it will on the next one. You can ask questions in a leading way in order to get the customer moving in your direction. "If you were going to buy this car, do you think you would buy the red one or the black one?" Simply changing how you approach the customer gets them thinking positively about your product and essentially making a decision without you being arrogant.

In my opinion, people try to cover their lack of self-confidence through arrogance. To avoid being arrogant you must first be comfortable with who you are as a businessperson. If you don't have confidence in your ability or training, you may try to cover up inadequacies by being arrogant. If you don't believe in your product you may react in the same way. We circle back to being self-aware; once again, this is an attribute that is so very important and needs to be fostered. If you find yourself avoiding a certain customer or one of your product lines, I would bet there is something deep down that you are questioning about yourself or your product. You have to be able to give yourself an honest evaluation and realize what is holding you back. If you can't figure it out, it is up to you to reach out to a mentor or trusted colleague for their input. Once you have recognized the problem, you should take advantage of the resources at your disposal to address the problem. Until you are confident in yourself, it will be extremely challenging to be a successful salesperson.

The other place that arrogance rears its ugly head is when people are interviewing for jobs. I have sat on both sides of the desk when it comes to interviewing and if someone is not genuine or does not come prepared for an interview, I think it is a complete slap in the face. There are many managers whose interview style is to make people as uncomfortable as possible to see if the interviewee will stick to their story and show that they truly believe their answers. You will also go through interview processes in which different interviewers at different levels of responsibility will ask you the same question a number of times. They do this for two reasons, the first is to make sure you are telling the same stories and not making up answers. The second is to see if they can get you to back off of your proclamations as the pressure increases. Confidence is king in the sales and interview process, but in order to truly be confident, you must be self-aware and confident in the person you are. If you are confident, no one will be able to back you off of your convictions. If you hold your ground in a respectful manner your customer will be confident in you, which is the key to a long and productive business relationship.

# 21

## *Tip Appropriately*

I believe in tipping; maybe it is because I have had jobs in my life in which I depended on tips and was constantly surprised by people's poor tipping habits. I believe that good tipping involves the correct amount and consistency, not just arbitrary money left behind. I also believe that tipping appropriately will take you a long way in the bar and business world. The key is not going overboard and making sure that you don't disappoint by shorting them and pulling the old "I'll get you next time." Consistency in tipping is critically important, especially when it comes to the business world. If people expect praise because you constantly hand it out and then all of a sudden you stop, you can be sure people on your team will become concerned over your newly found frugality with gratitude.

I feel very strongly that there is a minimum of 25% when it comes to tipping. I don't care how bad the service was and how slow they were with the drinks; I always will tip the bartender a quarter of the bill. For one, I think that tipping is good for the soul. I feel that by tipping a low-performing waiter or bartender, you show the class that your server didn't show you. I like to think that they will learn something from you and try better next time. Perhaps it is wishful thinking, but what can I say, I am an optimist. Over-tipping also creates challenges. Of course, your server will enjoy your 150% tip, but it sets a tough precedent to live up. Tip appropriately and consistently. The only times in my life when I have broken this rule is when I have had the contact at the bar that covered my bill. In that case, I have tipped the amount that I thought the bar tab would have been. When it comes to praise and thanks with a customer, I follow similar rules. I always thank my customers for an appointment time and definitely for orders. I never go overboard with my thanks and praise of a customer or colleague. "Oh my God, that is the most brilliant idea, I have ever heard. What would this organization be without you and your ideas?" or "Thank you so much for ordering my product; it was amazing to watch you work through the negotiating process. I feel like I am a better person by going through this process with you." Does either of these sound like a sincere compliment or thank you? No, they are lip service and completely over the top in my view. There is no way you will be taken seriously by the person on the other end of these grandiose statements. You will be seen as completely disingenuous or worse, desperate. You come off as a kiss ass, and no one respects a kiss ass. This is a point often missed by those looking to climb the corporate ladder. No worthwhile individual wants to be sucked up to and "yessed to death." I have made a fair living respectfully and tactically pushing back on my management when the time is appropriate. You don't move forward in an organization by sucking up, you earn leadership positions by being a team member of substance.

All I am really saying is to be sincere and grateful. You definitely need to say thank you and give praise when it is appropriate, and when it comes to thank you, it is always appropriate. You must say thank you for an order, an appointment, or even just some good information from your customer. When a colleague goes above and beyond for you or has a big win, it is appropriate to give them the appropriate level of praise. Most of the time, a firm handshake and thank you or good job is all that you need to show someone that they are appreciated or did a great job. If someone really made a huge commitment to you in the form of a huge sale or someone really went above and beyond to help you, a modest gift is appropriate. When I say modest, I mean a meal, drinks, or perhaps a personalized gift that will be a memento of what was accomplished. Showering a customer with gifts sets a dangerous precedent. If the customer comes to expect it, what happens when the budget dries up and the gifts go away? Will that customer's level of disappointment drive them to another vendor? I don't want to be in the position to find out. I always thank my customers for orders, but the way I see it I have given as much to them as they have to me. I have brought a product or service that will increase their profitability and efficiency. In a way, we are now "friends with benefits." We both are getting something out of the relationship but can move on to another project when we feel appropriate. One other issue with showering people with praise and gifts is that you give away any power position you had in the relationship. If you have to kiss ass to get anything done, you will never be able to play hardball with that customer. Remember, when you sell you are building a business relationship, not a personal relationship. In order to keep the relationship business and not personal, you must always have to maintain a bit of distance between you and your customer. Remember that you are a person of substance and showed the customer significant value in your product, so keep the praise and thanks at an appropriate level and you will be better off in the long run.

For those of you reading this book who are under the age of 40, I would like to remind you that a proper thank you note is on paper, not an email or text message. Please, please go out and buy some thank you notes. If you want to go all out, you can even get some personalized thank you cards and envelopes. When you interview, it is fine to send an email, but make sure you send a handwritten note that gives them a very simple thank you and that you are excited about the opportunity. When a customer places an order, send them a handwritten note thanking them for their business and that you are excited to work together. I once went into the General Manager of North America's office and what did I see openly displayed? A handwritten thank you note following a trip he made to see one of my customers. Below it, I saw the thank you note I wrote him after he promoted me with about 10 other handwritten notes from some of my colleagues. This man received literally hundreds of emails on a daily basis and some of them were likely thank you emails; my guess is he deleted them and moved on with his day. Those dozen or so handwritten notes stayed on the corner of his desk for at least a year based on when I sent my first note. The handwritten note is a lost art; you need to learn how to master it and use it to your benefit. Take the time to address an envelope, write the note, put a stamp on it, and place it in a mailbox. I know we don't receive mail too often these days, but for any of you who remember waiting for a non-Prime package, gift, or letter to arrive, you know how exciting it is to see something addressed to you, that someone took the time to write and mail. Handwritten notes are worth their weight in gold, and I promise they will distinguish you from the rest of the crowd.

To sum it up, don't be a kiss ass, but do be grateful and sincere when dealing with colleagues and customers. Do not hesitate to give out thanks and praise early and often but do it at an appropriate level. If you take it too far you will lose the respect of the people you sell to and work with. Be consistent; if you express gratitude verbally, please make sure you do so without fail across the board, or you run the risk of people thinking they did something wrong when they aren't praised for something you previously would recognize. If you are not prone to give our praise easily, then don't, but be sure to recognize when someone goes above and beyond. My grandfather was the kind of guy who never gave out much praise; if you got straight As, he would ask, "Why aren't they A+s?" This is a very old-school approach that may or may not work in this day and age. However, there is one benefit to being prudent with your praise. When you do recognize someone, they will know just how special it is to be called out. When that same grandfather would tell me, I had a great game, I know how truly special it must have been. When it comes to tipping, I am more of the "praise early and often" school of thought, and I have no issue staying consistent in this regard. It is up to you to decide which style works best for your personality. Regardless of how often you give praise, just remember to stay sincere and consistent.

# 22

## *Close Out Your Tab*

Have you ever had a big night out and mistakenly left your credit card at the bar without closing out your tab? I hate when this happens, and the following morning is the worst part of the whole episode. You don't realize that you have left your card until you are out buying coffee or breakfast the next day. Once you realize you are without your plastic, you have to wait for the bar to open and hope that the card is actually still there and not maxed out. It never fails that the bartender who over-served you is there the next day and gives you the "you were a mess last night" look. They have already charged the card, wrote in a 25% tip and you now have a sour taste in your mouth about the night before. The worst part is the person you are most frustrated with is yourself! A lot of salespeople like to quote *Glengarry Glen Ross*, "A.B.C.; always be closing"; it is a great scene, and although I agree with the premise, very few people truly close properly. There are two likely scenarios when it comes to ineffective closing. The first is they close without actually demonstrating any value. The second is they completely forgot or don't have enough confidence to close at all.

There are entire books on the subject of closing, I will only give you a few pages, but I would like you to keep one thing in mind. You will never have a particular moment back ever again, you may be able to go back to the same bar or get a chance to win the deal again, but each moment or night out is unique and fleeting. With this in mind, you have to take advantage of each situation to your fullest capability, every time. You don't have to hit a home run with each attempt to close, but you do have to close as aggressively as possible. Just think it through, if you are in an introductory meeting it is probably not the time to ask for the whole ball of wax. You definitely need to gain some level of commitment from the customer, and you should try to push it as much as possible, but sometimes just securing

DOI: 10.4324/9781003218258-22

a second meeting is the best close that is possible. A close can also be as simple as just establishing action items for you and your customer. The key is that when you have the opportunity to close, do it or you are essentially leaving the bar without closing out your tab. If you do not close, you have let go of all control in the deal, similar to when your credit card is sitting at the bar as the bar closes. You did all of the work that you could do, you gave your presentation, spoke about the features and benefits, and gave your customer every reason to buy your product, but you forgot to ask them to do something for your benefit. I could talk about closing all day, but the key is to close appropriately and make sure that you do it every time you meet with your customer.

Let me pose another question to you, when the bartender slides your tab across the bar you pay it, right? Of course, you do, but do you ever pay the tab a second time? Even better, do you ever have the bartender run 70% of the tab and then the bartender run the card again for the last 30%? Of course you don't, when you close your tab, you close the whole thing. I know that this premise is a bit absurd, but this is exactly what the majority of salespeople do on a daily basis. They close halfway because it is easier than asking for everything, or they fail to recognize the opportunity that is literally slapping them in the face. If your close seems too easy, then it is my guess that you have not asked for enough from your customer. As a general rule, never want to close your tab twice. Once you close and get the answer you want from your customer, walk away. You don't need to have the customer buy the same product twice so don't close them twice. On a similar note, I would try to avoid a second close when you have not asked for enough from your customer. If you have only closed 75% of the way, you most likely will not have the chance to close the rest of the way with your customer. It is worth a probe if you find yourself in this situation: "Is there any other need that you need to address? What are your thoughts on bundling this solution into a larger deal?" You have to make the effort if your close comes up short, but it is always better to ask for all the business that is there the first time around, the worst thing you will get is pushback.

The good news is when the customer pushes back, you have an opportunity to learn. If you are making steady progress through the sales process and you have a high level of confidence you can win most or a large portion of the deal, that is the time to push on the customer. I always like to confirm closes in writing after getting the verbal buy-in. I will usually address the client with excitement about the future and how

I look forward to working with them. Then, I will summarize the close in detail. This should not come as a surprise to the customer, as they have already accepted, but there is always something lost in the translation and time can often be your enemy. If the client does not agree with the action items or terms, they will certainly let you know, most people are much looser with their spoken work than their written word and any nuance with their customer or process will come through a clearly defined close and timelines. Once you have the issues on the table, you can address them; whether it is a process or people issue, you have learned something through your effective close.

Closing is an art, and you have to be able to read the person sitting across the desk from you and close appropriately. Even though it is an art and can't be forced, there are a few rules that I follow when it comes to closing. First, not all closes come at the end of the conversation; when the opportunity to close presents itself, take it and then move on to the next point in your agenda. Second, no matter how small the close is, make sure you and the customer walk away from the meeting with commitments on both of your ends and that there is a clearly defined timeline for their completion. Third, close appropriately, meaning that you need to have a good measure of the person you are selling to, and you should have a best case and acceptable goal in mind before you enter the meeting. You have to at least walk away with the acceptable result even if you have more selling to do. Finally, don't be a force or rush a close. You must ensure that you have sold the product or service thoroughly before you even think about closing. Just remember, the close can be small in scale so even though you have to close, you must remember that there are multiple steps that you have to complete. Make sure that you actually sell something before you ask the customer to make a commitment. Finally, I would say don't be nervous about closing. This is where your level of confidence is critically important. If you have presented value to your prospect, the close should be the easiest part of the process.

# 23

## Send Pictures

One of the greatest innovations that came about when I was a teenager was the disposable camera. In the age of cell phone cameras, they have become completely obsolete, but back in the day they were a game-changer. It was cheap, easy to use, and enabled you to capture what had transpired that evening without any major headaches. This evolved into camera phones, Facebook, YouTube, Twitter, Instagram, etc. Now it seems like anything that anyone has done anywhere in the world is captured and stored somewhere. I have to admit I still have picture albums of pictures from my college and high school years. I probably haven't looked at them in 10 years, but I still have them, and I definitely remember the stories that are associated with all of those pictures. I am sure some of you have this type of memorabilia as well, but I sincerely hope that you don't bring them out on a regular basis. If you do, it is time to move on and grow up a little bit. It is important to look fondly on good times and the people who were there to share in those good times. As a matter of fact, I still try to get fun and interesting pictures out to my friends after we hang out. Although I don't have too many wild nights out anymore, if I actually make it past midnight it is a small miracle. When dealing with clients, you must give them good "visuals" as well. Your customer should be reminded about the good times along with the tough times and how you worked through them together. It is important to remember the experiences that you have had with your customers, both good and bad. It gives you both a point of reference and, hopefully, lessons learned, allowing your next deal to work out even better for you both. However, there must be a balance of the past, present, and future. It is important to not live in the past, while not completely dismissing it.

When you are working with customers it is important to talk about both past successes and challenges. When it is a repeat customer, you need to

DOI: 10.4324/9781003218258-23

make sure to highlight the positives of your last project. Don't assume the customer will remember what you did for them, they will almost certainly forget something that you did that was vital to your mutual success. Putting these positive thoughts in your customer's head will reassure them and give your client the sense of security that they desire when making an investment. It is also important to acknowledge the challenges that were encountered in the past and how you handled them. If you didn't handle this properly in the past, winning the next deal will be that much harder. However, you must take this on and tell the customer your specific plan for how and why this experience will be better and make up for the past mistakes. If you are fortunate enough to get a second chance, you better come through in a big way or you will lose a customer for life. When you are working with a new customer you must walk a fine line of the past, present, and future. You need to give examples of other clients and how they have been happy with your product or service, but you can't make it all about some other customer. If you are meeting a girl or guy at the bar, they sure as hell are not interested in hearing how great your last relationship was, tell new customers who you work with and how it has been successful, and then move on to the present. Ask a lot of questions about the present; it is important to not act like you know exactly what is going on within your customer's organization. Use your past experiences to recognize the best solution for this new customer and then tailor the message for your product or service to the new company's needs. It seems like an oxymoron to focus on the future while keeping the past fresh in your mind, but you must use the past to plan for the future. The worst thing you can do is make the same mistake twice. First, it is completely avoidable; second, it makes you look foolish within your organization and in front of your customer. Just remember, even if you had a difficult few days or weeks with a customer in the past, you can still win. If you were able to make it through the difficult times and still accomplish the goal, you are truly of value to the customer. Anyone can sell when things are rosy, the A players can sell when things are a disaster. When I referenced placing a value on you as well as your product, it was in an effort to give you that edge when battling with your competitors. If all things are equal, and you have demonstrated an ability to manage through the tough spots while being a part of the good times as a partner with your customer, you will certainly be well-positioned to win competitive deals as the incumbent. Again, this sort of sweat equity is not easy to attain and very easy to lose, so stay on your toes.

It is also important to set a reasonable expectation for your customer; just remember there is never a perfect party or deal. I have been promised the VIP treatment many times before in a social setting. Sometimes the people come through, most of the time, I am extremely disappointed in our "hook up" and that free tab that I was promised costs me a few hundred dollars. Make sure you tell your customer the good as well as the bad, or more specifically the areas of development about your product or service. If you have weak points to your product, make sure that you also have solutions to remedy the issues for your prospective customer. You don't have to focus on the negative, but you have to acknowledge things like additional construction costs or licensing issues. Once you manage through your client's initial feedback on this weak point, you will gain credibility with the customer. In this case, you give the customer a better and more complete picture of how the deal will go down from start to finish. This is called a plan. If you have a fully baked plan, the bumps in the road that we always experience will be easier to handle. If you promise the stars and deliver the moon, you will never allow your product or service to be truly appreciated. You could have the world's greatest mousetrap, but if you tell your customer that it will also boil an egg, your customer will never appreciate the greatness of your mousetrap. Unrealistic expectations are like an anchor for your product. No matter how good your device is at the stated goal, the unreasonable expectation you set will hold you back in your customer's eyes. Sing the praises of what your product or service does, but make sure that you don't over-promise. When you make commitments to your customer that you are not able to fulfill, it equates to lying to your client, which is always a recipe for disaster.

I used to work on the road the vast majority of the time, so I didn't have an office I worked from every day. Now that we are in the age of Zoom and Teams calls, my home office has become a much larger point of focus. My home office has multiple pictures of family and friends to remind me why I go to work every day. It also shows my clients that I am more than just an empty suit (or half of a suit on video calls). When I do actually get out on the road, my cell phone pictures remind me of the people for whom I truly work every day. The pictures I see of family and friends calm me down when I am fired up. It keeps me focused when my mind is wondering, and it definitely reminds me why I am out there grinding. As a general rule, people tend to do more for those who are on the top of their minds. I know that when I saw my friends after quarantine and vaccination, I found myself doing more to help or see them again. In business, there are times that "sending a picture" is just being a consistent presence with your customer. There have been thousands of books about selling and business, but to be perfectly honest 95% of this rat race is just being in front of the customer at the right time. It is tough to predict when the right time is, so you have to be a fairly regular presence with your customer even if there is no pending business. In some ways, it is more important to be in front of the customer when there is nothing pending. It shows that you have a true appreciation for what the customer does and that you aren't just a Johnny come lately. Nobody likes the guy who only shows up when it is an open bar; make sure that you aren't the salesperson who is a ghost in between sales or RFPs. You may be saying, "This is an easy one, of course I will be a presence in between deals." I will tell you that this becomes very difficult the more success you achieve. If you are only selling to a few people, it is easy to be there all of the time. When you start breaking through and selling to fifty, a hundred, or a thousand customers, it is impossible to be a constant presence for all of your customers. You can keep in touch via phone or email if you can't be there in person. The important thing is to make sure that you are making an effort to see your customers regularly. Your clients will recognize that you are busy because you are selling so much, which will reassure them that they are working with the right salesperson. They will also recognize whether you are showing gratitude outside of the deal process, and if they feel taken for granted, you will have some fences to mend. If make sure you are fresh in your customer's mind and you will have an advantage over all of your competitors. In order to do this, you must make an effort to be consistent.

# 24

## Recover

When the day is done, you need to be able to shut it down and turn work off for at least 8 hours or so. This sounds easy, until you try and put it into practice. I personally struggle with this regularly and have certainly shorted my family some well-deserved time over the years, but I strive to get better! I am sure you all can think of a friend who needs to spend a few less nights out at the bar and a few more nights in watching a movie. This person was probably the life of the party when you all were a little younger. Their antics were hilarious, and you truly wanted to spend time around them due to their pleasant disposition and willingness to have fun at all costs. However, as the years went by, your friend stayed on the same schedule of going out and although their antics are still amusing, you can now only take them in small doses. Overworking yourself can produce diminishing and then negative returns over time. There must be a safe space or release activity that separates you from your work. You need to make sure you have time away from the sales world in order to maintain your level of productivity. You also have to allow your customers time to recover, or you run the risk of alienating them. The constant "full court press" of your clients will actually lead them to avoid you, no matter how good you and your product are, because you are simply grinding them down.

I really don't care what it is that you do to get away from work as long as it doesn't cause you or your family harm. Having already mentioned my struggle with this mindset, I have gotten better over the years. It is time I spend with my family and golf that provides me a release from the stress and pressure of my work life. My family brings everything into perspective when it comes to work. "I need to get to that email, actually I really don't. There is nothing that can be done about this situation at 9:30 at night." It

DOI: 10.4324/9781003218258-24

is very important that you realize you have to put in the work and keep your focus on the customer. However, you need to turn off work and the thoughts about work once you have finished that day's work. To be clear, I am not telling you to ignore work when the clock hits 5 pm. Salespeople do not punch a time clock for a reason and when serious issues arise, you need to be responsive to your customer and the situation. However, even in times of crisis, you have to flip the switch to "off" and resume the hard work the next day. Please do not be a slave to your phone or computer 16 hours a day or on holidays and weekends. Unless there is something truly disastrous that is going on, chances are it can wait until Monday morning. Even if I have a tremendous amount of work to do, I still try to make sure that I give my help with bath and bedtime with my kids when I am not traveling. I will put my work off until after my family time is done so I can at least say that I was there to tell my kids good night and that I love them. The email that is waiting in my inbox will not self-destruct in 30 seconds and will be there when it is time to do work. If it is an emergency someone will pick up the phone and call you.

Golf is another release for me, but in a different way. Golf allows me to compete outside of work, which I feel is critically important. Competing at work is serious business, I won't say it is life and death, but it is much more serious than how I compete on the golf course. Losing a golf match stings, but it does not affect my family like losing a big client or deal. Maybe you play in a basketball league or do landscaping as a release, whatever it is make sure you prioritize some "me time." You can and should take your selected pastime seriously, but it should never be so serious that affects your work. This type of time away can net big gains for you in the future, and in my opinion is a requirement to avoid burnout. Just remember, recovery time is something that is supposed to rejuvenate you and should be a positive in your life, not a negative. If your release is polishing off a bottle of vodka, I would suggest that your release is not a healthy one. It is like being hungover from a big night and deciding the best recovery method is ten beers. The hair of the dog may make you feel better in the short term, but there will be detrimental effects to you over the long term.

I remember when I first started in sales; I would sit by my computer at night and hope that an email would come through so I could show my bosses that I was working harder than anyone else. I still have the tendency to do work when I shouldn't; sometimes it is just easier to take 15 seconds to answer a simple question from my phone. So, there is a little do as I say, not as I do in this chapter, but I can honestly say that the older I get, the easier it is to carve out some recovery time for myself. The problem with staying on a constant grind is at some point you begin to make simple mistakes and your productivity suffers. If you refuse to take a break when you notice your productivity slipping, you will eventually make so many mistakes and the losses will outpace the wins. And let's not mince words here; this type of activity is flat-out unhealthy. I have seen many people end up in the hospital as a direct result of stress and not being able to put it in neutral. Some people have told me that sales are their passion and that their release is sales. I find this a bit disingenuous, but if this is the case for you, I would suggest that your release would be to still take a break from your deals and study the art of selling without grinding on your own situation. If you constantly worry about every deal and add unneeded pressure to an already stressful situation, you will eventually paralyze yourself.

One of the many things that make business tough is that you are dependent on the decision of someone else for your livelihood. As a result, some salespeople will tend to smother their customers. Please remember, the customer will need some recovery time as well and you have to give them a break from time to time. Try to put yourself in their shoes. The customer has an important job to do that has nothing to do with buying from you. The customer has to manage their people, fight off their own competitors and stay on the cutting edge of technology while trying to satisfy their own customer's needs. When customers buy from you, they give you their precious time and money; you need to respect that they have a lot more on their plate than you. A common mistake I see is salespeople who make the deal all about themselves and not the customer. "I really need this deal to hit my quota this month" is not going to truly motivate your customer to cut you a purchase order. No matter how good your relationship is, that customer's priority is their business, not yours. You need to respect the customers' time and give them the appropriate amount of thanks when appropriate. I am not in favor of short-term gains at the expense of the future, but if you need to pull a deal into this quarter, make sure you are giving the customer a better motivator than helping you out. You can only visit that well a time or two before your customer will become disenchanted with your constant for a favor.

Once the customer has bought from you, they will expect you to follow up thoroughly on the product or service, so that is your first priority.

Even after you have met or exceeded all customer expectations, you still need to give your customer some recovery time before you start to push them into another sale. In an ideal world and if you have sold properly up front, you should have a plan for the future with specific timelines in mind that your customer has committed to and is invested in. Being that the world is usually not ideal, you will have to battle for that next book of business, but it is important to be respectful of the time and money your customer will have to invest in their next purchase. There will be times when your customer will drag their feet when you have a solution that will save them tremendous time and money, it is important to respect their process and intelligently position your next sale. Patience is required here and although it is against my nature, sometimes you just have to wait. It can start with simply asking the customer in passing what else is on their agenda? I will make subtle comments about another customer who bought your new product and what it has done for their profit margin and productivity. Give the customer small teases on what your product can do for them. Author Josh Metcalf calls this "pounding the stone." The moral of the story is there is no one swing of the hammer that actually breaks the stone. The stone breaks on the last of what is many swings and each of the hits equally contributes toward reaching your goal of cracking that stone. Passing comments, questions about your customer's goals, and just showing up to support your customer are the number of hits that you make on your "stone" or client before you break through. It requires patience, clarity of purpose, and confidence in your abilities, which are all critical for success in business.

Often, there is no set time or process for when your customer is ready for their next purchase. As a sales professional you must stay close without being overbearing and when the customer starts giving you buying signals, take advantage as the incumbent. Here is one way to approach the next deal: "It has been a pleasure working with you and your team as my company's product has gone from a proposal to a reality. Your team has been pleased with the product, is more productive, and your profits are up. Normally I would say my job is done here, but I have another solution that has shown a 10% marginal increase with clients in similar markets. Now this new offering does come at a price, and my goal would be to provide solutions that continue to be valuable to your company with tangible results. When are you available to discuss this product in more detail?" You may want to say this in a different way, but the heart of the message should remain. Highlight what you and your product have done in the past and why your customer needs to come out of pocket again. Receiving pushback here is not a bad thing; pushback is something we can learn from. If your customer is not ready or doesn't have the money to buy, they will most certainly let you know and if they ignore you, that is a no! This brings us back to patience and process. You must be willing then to wait and let the customer recognize the value of your next product and then work with them to get the deal across the finish line as a team, not as you being a nuisance. You can rarely "annoy" a customer into buying and if you are fortunate enough to do it once, there won't be a second time.

# 25

## Know When It's "That Time"

At some point in most of our lives there is an incident or an unusually rough morning where we think, "next time I'm staying home to watch a movie." It happens to all of us, you can't keep the same pace up and you're tired of seeing the same crowd every weekend, or you're simply looking for a new adventure. Whether it be the right significant other in your personal life or an amazing opportunity at work, what excites us changes over time. It is important to embrace this change with understanding that it is a very normal part of your personal development.

When it comes to your profession, you will also come to crossroads at many points in your career. Maybe you want to move into a management role, marketing, operations, or maybe something you have zero experience in right now. On the other side of the coin, you may come to the point where you dread going to bed, because you know you have to wake up and go to your job the next day. Our mind and body will tell us when it's time to make a change, embrace it as this is not something to be feared. I can say with all confidence that if you are not enjoying your day-to-day activity, the pay and the title that come with your job don't matter. Hanging on to "the good old days" is a recipe for failure and regression as a person and a professional. There are few things sadder than watching a once highly performing businessperson slide into complacency. Complacency is something that you should fight tooth and nail on a daily basis. Please understand that this has nothing to do with promotions career advancement. You can stay in the same role for 30 years and not become complacent. Complacency to me is not being moved by positive or negative results and the best way I visualize this is the shoulder shrug. It tells me that you don't really care what happens either way, and you have accepted that your results will be determined by fate and not your ability.

DOI: 10.4324/9781003218258-25

In order to break this cycle, you must seek out change for the better every day. I am not telling you to change for change's sake; what I am really saying is make sure you step out of your comfort zone as many times as possible on a daily basis. Change is hard, and often frightening; if you take on change with positivity and energy, you will experience a period of hyper-growth that will take you to heights that seem unachievable today. All of us default back to what is comfortable from time to time; the key is not relying on your comfort zone.

My first manager at Pfizer would come on "ride alongs" with me often. It's not because I was special, he had to, it was his job. After a few months of really getting comfortable with my products, territory, and customers he came for a typical day in the field with me. We saw a variety of customers that day, and I was spot on with my messaging all day. Not a missed word or mishandled visual aid all day. As you can imagine, I felt quite confident when I pulled into the McDonald's parking lot where he left his car for the day. I was expecting him to tell me how great I was, how I absolutely crushed it that day, and that if I continued on this trajectory, I would be promoted in record time. I was giddy with anticipation as I put my company-issued Chevrolet Impala into park. What came next was quite unexpected. He asked, "How do you think you did today?" I responded with a resounding "Great! I was on message all day and hit all the points we discussed at the last POA." He followed up with, "So, you were comfortable all day?" I responded with a resounding "Definitely." "Well, if that is the case, you didn't do your job today," he said. I was dumbfounded; I thought, "What is he talking about? I crushed it today! I hit every point there is to hit and my customers responded just as I expected." My manager went on to crush my soul a bit, and it has ended up being a positive for me as soon as I recovered. In short, his lesson was if I was in my comfort zone all day, I hadn't challenged myself and more importantly, my customer to do anything differently than I have been. Please remember, we are in the business of changing habits to benefit the customer, the customer's customer, and the organization for which I work. If you are always comfortable, you have become complacent, and it is certainly "that time" for you.

When it's "that time" you will see what you do on a daily basis in a different light, it may seem monotonous or easy. Don't fall victim to thinking you know it all, keep learning, working, and staying positive. Your next challenge will come with many unknowns, if you stay humble, yet aggressive your transition will be a smooth one. Please seek out change wherever and whenever you can, hopefully in the form of new challenges. When you were growing up you did not want to be the best at being comfortable, you wanted to excel and reach your peak performance or beyond. For some of us, it was athletics, others wanted to be a world-renowned doctor or a wildly successful trial attorney. Now that you are older, your career path probably isn't what you were expecting when you were a kid, but that burning desire to perform at the highest level possible remains. Don't settle for comfortable, strive to reach beyond your comfort zone, and good, yet hard, things will follow.

One point of caution once you have begun embracing change. Be smart enough to know what you don't know. I have worked for and with far too many people who thought they needed to have all the answers, at all times. Let's say you have been promoted, which means you were very good at your old job and your management feels you have transferable skills that could lead to success in a position higher on the food chain. This does not mean you know it all. It does mean that you should arrive in your new role with a certain level of humility. You should still be confident, but you should do more listening than talking and when you are overwhelmed, ask for help.

Many people think that asking for help is a sign of weakness; it is not. Understanding where you have knowledge gaps and asking others with this expertise is one of the most confident and competent things a businessperson can do. Just be sure that you have stretched to the outer reaches of your knowledge base, because asking someone else to do a job that you are capable of doing is textbook complacency.

Breaking out of your comfort zone may often come with a change of employer, which under most circumstances is perfectly acceptable. Just be sure that you are running toward an opportunity and not running away from issues in your previous role. The world is small and leaving scorched earth behind is always bad policy. There is nearly a 100% chance that you will work for or with a former colleague, and they will remember how you left the previous company. Be a grown-up, take care of your business, and seek your new opportunity with vigor, while remembering the lessons and people from your previous role.

Recognizing when it's "that time" is not an exact science and your pursuit of change should be done in a measured way. Please make sure you keep an eye out for complacency, it is having toxic effects on you and your career arc. Once you find the next challenge, pursue it with everything you have and don't look back. There will be haters and doubters along the way, you must trust yourself above any other person. Your belief is the thing that will carry you through to success. Being self-aware is critical through times of change, and you will need to do near constant self-check-ins to see if you are displaying confidence and not arrogance, to make sure you are reaching out and listening to the locals, and that you understand your time and place along the way. Don't be nervous about asking for help, it is a sign of strength, not weakness. Most importantly, you must be honest with yourself and your customers. If you can go down this check all of these boxes, I can honestly say that you are on the correct path. However, you are not all the way there yet, and I know this because life and business are about constant evolution and improvement. If you feel you have arrived and there is nothing more to accomplish, I suggest you go seek out a new challenge. Trust me, they are out there, you just have to accept them.

# Takeaway

After six years of writing, editing, and proofing this book, it became clear that there is a certain level of common sense that permeates this theory, which I truly believe speaks to its credibility. It is okay to be skeptical, I have questioned every sales theory or training I have ever received. My request is that you keep an open mind and put some or all of these thoughts into use. I can honestly tell you that I have found at least one great technique from each seminar I have been a part of in my career, regardless of my skepticism.

If you avoid one pitfall, capitalize on one opportunity, obtain one piece of career-altering advice from a "local," or experience any other unintended, yet positive, outcome from reading these words, I have accomplished my goal.

Writing this was a tremendous personal experience and I hope that some of you who are just getting started or are looking for a new spark in your career have enjoyed reading it, and will put some of this advice into action. I have a passion for business and sales, and I wrote this to share what I have learned with people in search of help or additional insight. I will only ask that you quote this book frequently if you liked it, steal everything you can from it, and write to me with your stories.

The transition that is made to be a high-performing sales professional is the most exciting journey you will make in your career. I would echo the advice that I was given a long time ago to absorb every piece of information you can along the way. Enjoy the ride up the ladder of success and never forget your roots, and the worst thing you can become is arrogant. You can all enjoy success and when you do, please pass along your wisdom to the next generation.

I would wish you all luck, but you don't need it. Go out there and crush it!

# Index

Accountability, 37, 41
Agenda, 14–18, 44
Arrogance, 91–95

Bar Stool selling approach, 43–46
"Big" friends, 29–32, 60
Blackberry, 15
Board members, 9
Business/sales model, 22

Career change, 88
Career path, 85–88, 117
Center of attention, 53–55
CEO, 35, 68, 73
Challenges, 3, 48, 51, 58, 61, 105, 106,
    117, 118
Charisma, 53, 55
Check-the-box status update
    meeting, 14
Closing, 101–103
Comfort zone, 116, 117
Commitments, 38, 57, 67, 72, 101,
    103, 107
Competition, 25, 26, 34, 49, 50, 73,
    92, 93
Complacency, 115, 117
Confidence, 91–95, 102, 103, 112, 115
Conversations, 43–46
COO, 35
Credentialing process, 2, 3
Credibility, 2, 5, 10, 30, 39, 73, 107, 119
Crisis management, 62
C-suite, 4, 9
C-suite personnel, 2, 9
Customers, 1–4, 8, 13, 35
    convincing, 15
    needs, 19, 74, 111
    priority, 16, 111
    relations, 23
    requests, 26
    showering with gifts, 98
    timid, 18

Deal, 3–5, 8, 9, 23, 26, 27, 34, 38–40, 47, 48,
    71–73, 93, 101, 102, 106, 108, 111
Decision-making processes, 33, 34, 38
Discount, 18

Emotion, 45
Expectations, 71
Experiences, 75, 77, 105

Feedback, 59, 65, 107
Follow-up, 26, 93

Glengarry Glen Ross (film), 101
Goals, 14, 16, 17, 19, 26, 44, 69, 112
Gratitude, 99, 108

Help (Ask For), 117, 118

Internet, 2
Interview processes, 94, 95

Knowledge, 1, 2, 8, 73–76
Knowledge gaps, 117

Leadership, 30, 38, 73, 98
Listening, 44
Lombardi, Vince, 82
Lower-level workers, 9

Macroeconomics, 4
Managers, 21, 22, 29–32, 35, 82, 94
Metcalf, Josh, 112
Mid-level managers, 9, 10

Negotiations, 25, 73, 98
Network, 82
Non-negotiable rules, 34
Non-verbal signs, 46

Over-tipping, 97
Overworking, 109
The Oz Principle, 37

Patience, 112, 113
Pfizer, 116
Plan, 107
Positive thoughts, 105–106
Positivity, 62
"Pounding the stone," 112
Product review, 14
Product warranty, 11
Project manager, 38
Purchasing directors, 9

Recovery method, 109–113
Recovery time, 109–113
Relationships, 8–10, 31, 98–99
Request for Proposal (RFP), 7,
    58, 108
Respect, 33–36, 45, 59, 83, 111, 112
Responsibility, 37–41, 59, 72, 94
RFP, *see* Request for Proposal
Rules, 33, 34, 36, 65

Sales meetings, 81–83
Sales process, 102
Sales professionals, 3, 112, 119
Sales strategy, 81
Secondary supplier, 73
Self-aware, 88, 93–95, 118

Self-confidence, 45, 94
Self-deprivation, 49
Self-promotion, 30
Selling process, 43–46, 65
Selling strategies, 73, 81
"Settling down," 85–89
Smartphone, 15
Strategic planning, 3, 4
Strategic thinking, 3–5
Supply chain, 35

TCO, *see* Total cost of ownership
Thank you notes, 99
Time and place, 57–60
Tipping, 97–100
Total cost of ownership (TCO), 9
Training, 1, 32, 79, 81–82
Trust, 18, 29, 30, 34, 35, 46
Truth, 71, 72

UNICEF, 19

Value creation, 5, 8, 31
Valvano, Jim, 82
Vendors, 7, 18, 19, 33–35, 38

Weddings, 53–54

Printed in the United States
by Baker & Taylor Publisher Services